MUHAMMAD ALI
AND MALCOLM X

MUHAMMAD ALI AND MALCOLM X

THE FATAL FRIENDSHIP

A Young Readers Adaptation of *Blood Brothers: The Fatal Friendship Between Muhammad Ali and Malcolm X*

RANDY ROBERTS AND JOHNNY SMITH
ADAPTED BY MARGEAUX WESTON

Christy Ottaviano Books

LITTLE, BROWN AND COMPANY
New York Boston

Little, Brown and Company
Hachette Book Group
1290 Avenue of the Americas, New York, NY 10104
Visit us at LBYR.com

First Edition: October 2023

Little, Brown and Company is a division of Hachette Book Group, Inc. The Little, Brown name and logo are trademarks of Hachette Book Group, Inc.

The publisher is not responsible for websites (or their content) that are not owned by the publisher.

Little, Brown and Company books may be purchased in bulk for business, educational, or promotional use. For information, please contact your local bookseller or the Hachette Book Group Special Markets Department at special.markets@hbgusa.com.

Library of Congress Cataloging-in-Publication Data
Names: Roberts, Randy, 1951– author. | Smith, John Matthew. | Weston, Margeaux, author.
Title: Muhammad Ali and Malcolm X : the fatal friendship / Randy Roberts and Johnny Smith ; adapted by Margeaux Weston.
Other titles: Blood brothers (Young readers adaptation)
Description: First edition. | New York, NY : Little, Brown and Company, 2023. | "A Young Readers Adaptation of Blood Brothers : The Fatal Friendship Between Muhammad Ali and Malcolm X." | Includes bibliographical references and index. | Audience: Ages 9–13 | Summary: "Freshly adapted for young readers, this in-depth portrait showcases the complex bond between Muhammad Ali and Malcolm X, revealing how Malcolm aided in molding Cassius Clay into Muhammad Ali and helped him become an international symbol of Black pride and Black independence." —Provided by publisher.
Identifiers: LCCN 2022057179 | ISBN 9780316478854 (hardcover) | ISBN 9780316479080 (ebook)
Subjects: LCSH: Ali, Muhammad, 1942–2016—Friends and associates—Juvenile literature. | X, Malcolm, 1925–1965—Friends and associates—Juvenile literature. | African Americans—History—20th century—Juvenile literature. | Black Muslims—United States—History—20th century—Juvenile literature.
Classification: LCC GV1132.A44 R643 2023 | DDC 796.83092 [B]—dc23/eng/20230123
LC record available at https://lccn.loc.gov/2022057179

ISBNs: 978-0-316-47885-4 (hardcover), 978-0-316-47908-0 (ebook)

Printed in the United States of America

LSC-C

Printing 1, 2023

For my daughters, Alison and Kelly

—RR

For my daughter, Madison, the light of my life

—JS

For my sons, Carter, Amir, and Asher

—MW

CONTENTS

MUHAMMAD ALI
AND MALCOLM X

PROLOGUE

THE TRUTH

> Cassius [Clay] is in a better position than anyone else to restore a sense of racial pride to not only our people in this country, but all over the world.
>
> —*Malcolm X, 1964*

On February 25, 1964, Malcolm X knocked on a dressing room door in Miami. He eased into the tense room, exuding cool confidence on a night when his nervous young friend, a contender preparing for the biggest fight of his life, needed him more than ever. That night, Muhammad Ali thought about his opponent, the heavyweight champion of the world, Sonny Liston. Still known at the time by his given name, Cassius Clay, the handsome, charismatic braggart proudly boasted that he was the greatest boxer in the world. In the days leading up to the match, he had repeatedly taunted Sonny. He even predicted that he would knock out Sonny in the eighth round. But deep down, Cassius felt nervous because Sonny was one of the greatest heavyweight champions in history. Big and vicious, Sonny had injured many of his opponents, taking down some of the finest boxers in the world. Virtually no one, except Malcolm X and Cassius's younger brother, Rudy, believed he could survive the match. Almost every reporter covering the fight believed that Cassius Clay would need a miracle to save him from Sonny Liston's wrath.

Not many boxing fans worried about Cassius Clay's impending doom. He was far from popular, and hardly anyone considered him the next great sports hero. His "I am the greatest" routine had soured on everyone, after one too many proclamations. He was considered a poor sportsman for belittling opponents, insulting sportswriters, and praising himself.

Making matters worse in the eyes of the press and the public, Cassius had invited Malcolm X to Miami. A minister in the Nation of Islam, Malcolm was known as the spokesman for the "Black Muslims," a religious group that followed the teachings of their leader, Elijah Muhammad. As Black Nationalists, Malcolm and Elijah preached that the Nation of Islam should form a separate state exclusively for Black people and live independently from white Americans. The Nation of Islam did not support racial integration because the members knew all too well the long history of white supremacists attacking Black citizens. Integrating into society with white people, Malcolm thought, would only invite further acts of violence against them. There could be no peace between Black people and white people. Therefore, Malcolm believed, the races must separate. He said:

> If all of the token integration which you
> see in the South, and it's only tokenism,
> has caused the bloodshed that it has, what
> do you think white people, both North
> and South, will do on the basis of *real*
> integration?

Malcolm's controversial views about race relations and his presence in Cassius Clay's dressing room raised all sorts of political questions about the contender. Sportswriters suspected that Cassius had joined the Nation of Islam, and many feared that Black Nationalists would use Cassius to spread a dangerous message if he won the heavyweight championship. They saw Malcolm smiling at Cassius and whispering in his ear. They noticed how Cassius had adopted Malcolm's words, assumed his delivery, and embraced his regal body language. In some ways, Cassius had become a clone of his older mentor. Malcolm X was like the big brother he never had.

Soon reporters asked the obvious question: *Cassius, are you a Black Muslim?* The boxer didn't confirm that he had joined the Nation, but he certainly did not deny it. He spoke warmly about the Nation of Islam and affirmed that Malcolm X was his dear friend.

Since their first meeting in Detroit in 1962, Cassius and Malcolm had formed a brotherhood. In many ways, they seemed destined to grow close. Both men thrived being center stage, surrounded by an audience, whether at Malcolm's pulpit or in Cassius's ring. Neither one could resist a platform, an interview, or a debate. Both enjoyed sparring with words and manipulating the fears of opponents with sensational language. They were both fighters.

Before Cassius became Muhammad Ali, Malcolm saw something special in the young boxer that few others did. He recognized Cassius's intelligence and his unique ability to communicate with people. "Not many people know the quality of the mind he's got in there," the minister told a reporter shortly before Cassius's fight with Liston. Like Malcolm, Cassius was completely self-assured, defiant, and proud to be Black. He carried himself with confidence, boldly professing his own greatness with the same assertiveness that Malcolm used to denounce the crimes of white men.

Studying Cassius's interactions with reporters, and the way he captivated audiences with his performances, Malcolm realized that the contender could become something more than an athlete; he could be a voice for Black Power. If Cassius won the heavyweight crown, he would have the kind of far-reaching platform and influence that could unify Black people behind a political movement for freedom. But first Cassius would have to get over his own fears and beat Sonny Liston.

That's where Malcolm came in. Meeting in Cassius's dressing room before the fight, he reminded Cassius that Allah would protect him in the ring. Then, moments before the fight began that fateful February night, Malcolm X, Cassius Clay, and Rudy Clay faced east toward Mecca, Saudi Arabia—the Muslims' holy city—and bowed and prayed. They praised Allah and blessed his name. Afterward, Malcolm repeated a variation of what he had been saying since arriving in Miami. It was more prophecy than pep talk. He said:

This fight is the *truth*. It's the Cross and the Crescent fighting in a prize ring—for the first time. It's a modern Crusades—a Christian and a Muslim facing each other with television to beam it off Telstar for the whole world to see what happens! Do you think Allah has brought about all this intending for you to leave the ring as anything but the champion?

That moment was just the beginning of Cassius Clay's transformation into Muhammad Ali. Over the course of his relationship with Malcolm, the young boxer traveled across the country, visiting the Nation of Islam's mosques, maturing into a man influenced by the discontent in Black America and a movement that gave him an identity— a sense of self and racial pride. When the two men were together, especially in Miami and New York, Malcolm educated him about history, politics, and the wicked ways of the white man. Cassius Clay had long been a searcher, seeking answers to questions about the meaning of his life. Malcolm offered him a compass, a sense of direction in a chaotic world. The minister emboldened him to speak his mind and assert his freedom—to be himself, to be unapologetically Black. Malcolm's message empowered Cassius Clay to believe that he truly was the greatest.

Muhammad Ali and Malcolm X is the story of how Ali became the heavyweight champion, and the role Malcolm X played in his life as they both shook up the world. It's a tale of friendship and brotherhood, love and deep affection. It is also the story of deceit, betrayal, and violence—inside and outside the ring—during a climactic period of the fight for civil rights in America.

CHAPTER ONE

WHO WAS CASSIUS CLAY?

I'm gonna be the next heavyweight
champion of the world.

—Cassius Clay

Looking out the window of a segregated train car in December 1960, Cassius Marcellus Clay Jr. was headed from Louisville, Kentucky, to Miami, Florida. As the train traveled farther south, he saw miles of cotton and Confederate flags, a symbol of pride for white southerners and racism for Black people across the country. The South was ruled by the cotton industry and segregation laws that separated white and Black people.

Cassius was used to second-class treatment in America—after all, he'd grown up in segregated Kentucky—but as an Olympic medalist abroad in Rome, Cassius had experienced a freedom that he never had before. As a member of the United States Olympic team in 1960, he was a part of history. More specifically, he belonged to an elite group of Black American athletes who defied the odds and broke racial barriers. Decathlete Rafer Johnson, basketball star Oscar Robertson, track star Wilma Rudolph, and boxer Cassius Clay were the best in their sports. They dominated the Olympic games, breaking record after record, dazzling the world with their grace and talent as they led their teams and carried the American flag in the opening ceremonies. These Black heroes received the royal treatment. Italy was thousands of miles away from the segregated life they had experienced growing up in the United States. Returning home as champions, they were still treated as second-class citizens. Cassius quickly learned that he lived in two worlds: one where he was celebrated for being a good athlete, and one where he was dismissed based on the color of his skin.

At just eighteen years old, Cassius Clay arrived in Miami carrying two things: a beat-up suitcase and a big dream. At first glance, you'd assume the young man was a model. He was tall and slender, with a smooth baby face. But Cassius was a professional fighter. He had not only earned a gold medal in the Rome Olympics but also dazzled the press and fellow athletes with his charm and good looks. Now he set his sights on winning over the American boxing community, which was not a very welcoming group. Cassius would have to fight his way to the top. He recognized that Miami was just the first round.

Even though he had been treated like royalty in Rome, Cassius knew that in the Deep South, segregation defined nearly every facet of social life. Still, he held out hope. It didn't matter if people laughed or doubted him—the boxer had faith in himself. He thought becoming the best would make him rich and give him access to freedoms that Black Americans didn't have. He sensed he was destined to leave a mark on the world.

Cassius had moved to Miami to learn from some of the best trainers and boxers in the business at the 5th Street Gym. He didn't have any friends in this new town, which made it easy for him to get into a rhythm: *Train. Dream. Sleep. Repeat.* Each morning, Cassius jogged from his home in the Black section of town to the gym near the beach—the white section of town. He typically wore old blue jeans and worn-out combat boots. Cassius would talk to himself and shadowbox as he revved up for a full day of training.

Now, you may not think much of seeing someone running and talking to themself. You may even do this with your AirPods or headphones on. But this was 1960: A Black man in the South running around punching the air was bound to draw attention. And one day it did. A white police officer stopped Cassius, assuming he was up to no good. In response to the policeman's questioning, Cassius calmly shared his name and where he was going. The officer didn't believe him. Cassius even mentioned he was an Olympic gold medalist. Surely the officer would recognize the kid who had represented America on the world stage. The officer frowned. He was still suspicious. Cassius needed a white person to verify his testimony. Otherwise, he could be in big trouble.

Cassius must have feared the worst. He had grown up hearing stories about Black people who disappeared, were beaten, or were killed. His father, Cassius Clay Sr., told him about racist cops who had falsely arrested and brutalized Black folks. He warned Cassius and his brother, Rudy, about the many dangers outside their home: *Don't go into white people's stores. Don't leave our neighborhood. And don't get arrested.* In the 1950s, it was dangerous being a Black person. Mr. Clay was trying to protect his sons knowing there was little he could do if a white person, especially an officer, made accusations against them. He understood that if young Cassius or Rudy got arrested, they would be on their own. That nightmare scared him and many other Black parents, too.

Mr. Clay's haunting stories often emphasized brutality against Black people and how white supremacists were never punished for their crimes. For example, just a few years earlier, in 1955, a boy named Emmett Till was brutally murdered by racists in Mississippi for allegedly whistling at a white woman in a grocery market. In the Deep South, where the Ku Klux Klan reigned, Till's killers, two white men named Roy Bryant and J. W. Milam, were found not guilty by a jury of white men. It did not matter that there was enough evidence to convict them of murder. All that mattered to the jury was that Bryant and Milam were white men, and that meant that they would not be punished for killing a Black child. The story of Emmett Till left an impression on young Cassius. It was a reminder that there was no justice for Black people and that he could not trust the law to protect him. When he was a boy, Cassius would lie in bed at night and cry at the thought.

So, when he began training as a teenager in Miami, he knew all too well that there was little he could do to stop an aggressive white cop from harassing him. Fortunately for Cassius, when this happened, the officer called his trainer, Angelo Dundee. Cassius watched the policeman relax as Dundee confirmed he was one of his boxers: "That's Cassius Clay." The officer had never heard of him. In fact, he didn't really care. It reminded Cassius that being an Olympic athlete meant nothing here. In the South, he was just another Black man. This painful encounter became a powerful motivator. How could Cassius achieve international fame and still be treated like a second-class citizen? He wanted respect. He wanted everyone to know his name.

Cassius worked harder in the gym. He thought that becoming a heavyweight champion was the key to getting respect in America. He quickly made a name for himself in Dundee's gym, but it wasn't the name you'd expect. Many of the other boxers began calling him "big mouth." Cassius would taunt and talk to his opponents while he fought. He'd talk about their speed, their skills, or even their looks. If he were judged only by his confidence and ability to trash-talk, Cassius would have risen to the top almost immediately; but his boxing needed work.

At only 182 pounds, Cassius was considered a small heavyweight. Some trainers thought he should gain weight and adopt a heavy-hitting style. Dundee disagreed. After listening to Cassius talk and watching him spar, Dundee told his fighter, "Who you are is Cassius Marcellus Clay Jr., and that's the man I'm going to teach you to fight like. A guy is never going to get anywhere thinking he's somebody else." He appreciated that Cassius did not have to gain weight or mimic anyone else to become a champion—he just needed to work with his best assets: his hand and foot speed and his perception of distance. The trainer saw that Cassius was a different type of fighter, one who needed to feel that his opinion mattered, that he mattered. So, Dundee encouraged him. Dundee made sure to praise the fighter at every opportunity. Instead of barking orders *at* Cassius, Dundee spent time talking *to* him. He treated him like an equal—something Cassius appreciated. "I didn't train him," Dundee recalled. "I advised him."

With Dundee's support, Cassius spent hours at the gym, sweating in the run-down, smelly, termite-infested space. He didn't care about the state of the facility; he was focused on making moves. But every day, as he traveled to and from the gym, Cassius was reminded that,

outside the ring, he was just another Black face. While
he may have worked with people from all over the
world, he could live only in segregated Black neighborhoods. He would walk or jog home, sharing a friendly
smile or a quick hello with his neighbors. Cassius lived at
the Charles Hotel in the segregated part of Miami called
Overtown. The small hotel was poorly maintained, with
no air-conditioning in the sweltering Miami heat. To
make matters worse, lots of threatening folks hung out
right outside the hotel at night. Cassius didn't dare try to
make new friends. Any little altercation might ruin his
dream. He couldn't take the chance. So, he just stayed in
his room. For months, Cassius kept to himself. Far away
from home at just nineteen years old, Cassius was lonely.

Dundee's 5th Street Gym was not your ordinary boxing
gym. It wasn't fancy, but it was a place where talented
fighters pursued their dreams of becoming champions.
Many of the fighters came from Cuba, where Premier
Fidel Castro had recently outlawed professional boxing. There were English- and Spanish-speaking boxers,
all with a common goal. Many had escaped poverty and
even political persecution for a chance to become the
best. Each athlete felt that making it to the big leagues

was the ticket to respect. On 5th Street, everyone was equal. Everyone had a fighting chance.

Dundee's boxers were headed to big-time matches on a weekly basis. Several of the men he trained won championships. From lightweight to heavyweight titleholders, Dundee worked with the greatest boxers. And Cassius was at the center of all the action. Despite already being an Olympic gold medalist, he was just starting to make a name for himself in the competitive world of boxing. He fought new adversaries whenever he could and often received small payments after each win. His ego and energy filled every gym he entered. Soon, Cassius became known for his skills instead of his big mouth. News spread that a baby-faced kid from Kentucky had a cutting right hand. Dundee's training strategy was working. Sports reporters wanted to see the fast-moving, trash-talking star. And just as he did in Rome, Cassius seduced them with his charisma. He had his eyes on a big prize. He told everyone who'd listen that he was going to break the record for the youngest heavyweight champion of all time. Instead of laughing him off, people began to listen. Cassius clearly had a chance, but Dundee remained cautious. He knew that any misstep could not only hurt Cassius's career but also wound his self-esteem.

In February 1961, Cassius finally got his big break when a former world champion, Ingemar Johansson, arrived in Miami for a fight. Johansson was preparing to take on Floyd Patterson, the current titleholder and youngest heavyweight champion in history. He needed a sparring partner who could keep up with him. Guess who they picked? Cassius Clay.

This was Cassius's time to shine. Cassius kept chanting, "I'll go dancin' with Johansson." Sparring matches aren't usually large-crowd events, but Cassius was moving up in the ranks and people were eager to watch him work. Two thousand spectators sat in the crowd, ready to see what he could do.

With reporters and fans watching, Cassius almost felt as if he were back at the Olympics. He felt free. He felt respected. He felt he could beat Johansson—and he was right. Cassius danced around the ring as if he had wings, moving in circles, confusing his opponent. Ingemar Johansson was no amateur, but he wasn't very quick or good with his feet. Cassius hit him with light jabs, taunting him all the while by saying he didn't deserve to fight Patterson. Cassius's energy—along with his barbs—frustrated the boxer. Cassius dominated Johansson, forcing an abrupt ending to the fight after just two rounds. No one wanted a rookie to further embarrass the boxing star.

Cassius's dreams were coming true, but he couldn't avoid the world outside the gym. He moved to a better part of Miami but was still not allowed in certain hotels or on the beaches because of the color of his skin. And despite his rising fame, he continued to face racism. During a magazine interview with *Sports Illustrated*, Cassius and the photographer went shopping at a local store. The photographer took pictures of Cassius looking at clothes. As soon as a white employee saw him touching the merchandise, he told Cassius that Black people were not allowed to try on clothes. Back then, some white people thought that Black people were dirty. They would never buy clothes that a Black person had touched or tried on.

Cassius left the store immediately. He thought about living in two worlds again. The boxing ring was a world where he felt respected, but none of that mattered to people who couldn't see past his skin color.

In the late spring of 1961, Cassius moved into one of Miami's "Black hotels," the Sir John Hotel, which regularly welcomed celebrities such as Ella Fitzgerald, Louis

Armstrong, and Duke Ellington. Black stars had to stay there because Black people could not enter the city's finest hotels unless they were cooks, servants, or bellhops. Not even Joe Louis, America's most celebrated fighter as the heavyweight champion of the 1930s and 1940s, could check into the segregated luxury hotels on Miami Beach.

Cassius's new home was centrally located, near theaters and other entertainment. Fancier accommodations meant that Cassius was really moving up in his career, but he still enjoyed spending time with regular people. Cassius would go back to the Overtown neighborhood sometimes, where Black community members greeted him and made him feel welcome. Some even recognized him from the newspapers. Overtown's residents gave Cassius the respect he deserved. But even with adoring fans, Cassius realized he needed more. He was well on his way to accomplishing his dreams, but something critical was missing. He thought about how the Black people back home in Kentucky and right there in Overtown were treated. He remembered traveling through the Deep South, surrounded by Confederate flags. Cassius could not be truly fulfilled until everyone who looked like him felt that same freedom.

One day in Overtown, Cassius crossed paths with a

man standing in front of a building called Muhammad's Temple of Islam. The man waved him over and the two began talking. Cassius Clay introduced himself as he always did, "I'm gonna be the next heavyweight champion of the world." The stranger, named Sam Saxon, recognized Cassius and had actually been following his success since the Olympics. Cassius immediately connected with Saxon as a potential friend and noticed the newspaper he held was titled *Muhammad Speaks*.

He had heard about the publication before. In fact, he'd read it. A few years earlier, Cassius and his brother, Rudy, had taken a trip to Atlanta. There, they met a few members of the Nation of Islam—a Black religious group that practiced nontraditional Islam. They claimed to be Muslims, but the Nation of Islam was focused on Black Power. According to their doctrine, the "white man" was bad and could never change. They preached that Black people were the original people and through slavery had been stripped of their authentic names, culture, and language. Cassius had heard this philosophy before, but he was older now and curious. He wanted to know more about what it meant to be a Black man. He longed to feel pride about the color of his skin and to understand Black history. Deep down, who was Cassius Marcellus Clay Jr.?

Cassius began to spend time with Saxon and local members of the Nation of Islam at Miami's Temple No. 29, the makeshift mosque that housed the Nation's gatherings. A preacher taught Cassius that his name, his father's name, and his ancestors' names had all been chosen by their enslavers. They taught him that he was more powerful than he knew. They introduced him to their leader, the Honorable Elijah Muhammad, who proclaimed himself the Messenger because he believed he was sent from Allah to deliver the truth about the power of the Black race. The Nation of Islam answered Cassius's questions and encouraged his curiosity. Cassius had called himself "the greatest" before learning about Black history. After a few sessions with members of the Nation, there wasn't a doubt in his mind that he was, in fact, the greatest.

The more he learned about the Nation, the more he wanted to share the message of Black empowerment with others. Elijah Muhammad taught Cassius that being Black was never a bad thing; it was something to be proud of. He preached that Black people would one day rise up and take over the world, that they would no longer be second-class citizens. It all made sense to Cassius.

Growing up, he'd heard that everything black was bad and everything white was good. He couldn't understand why the heroic cowboys in movies always rode on white horses. He questioned why everyone on TV, from Santa Claus to Miss America, was white. Elijah Muhammad ingrained in him that Black was powerful, beautiful, and wise. As a young adult, Cassius finally understood that what he'd been taught was wrong. Cassius liked the idea of Black Power and finally getting some respect. Soon, he began faithfully attending the Nation of Islam meetings. He made friends in the organization and no longer felt so lonely in Miami.

Elijah Muhammad's doctrine was incredibly influential to Cassius: "The Black people in America have for many years been made to feel that they were something of a Divine Curse," he preached. "You must not think that about yourself anymore.... You are the Most Powerful, the Most Beautiful, and the Wisest." Cassius began to incorporate some of the Nation's teachings when he talked with friends or fellow boxers. He mentioned that Black people were a special group, and that their history was the greatest. Cassius even used the Nation's rhetoric in some interviews but was very careful not to reveal that he had been going to the Nation of Islam temple. Aligning himself publicly with any non-Christian religion could harm his future. He also knew that talking about

Black Power and the Nation's beliefs would make a whole lot of people uncomfortable.

Some of his friends and family were not supportive of this religious calling. Cassius's mother, Odessa, did not think the Nation of Islam was a good influence on her son. Close friends thought he was inventing tall tales. They told him "all that Black Power talk" was just a fantasy. But Cassius still believed. The teachings offered him a means of hope and survival in segregated America. The Nation of Islam taught Cassius that he was meant for greatness, and that soon things would change for Black people. Cassius needed to hear that.

The boxer began embracing the Nation of Islam, but Elijah Muhammad had doubts about him. Muhammad disapproved of sports, especially boxing, which he associated with gambling, drunkenness, and crime. But the local Muslim ministers believed Cassius was a good man and knew he was serious. In many ways, the Nation's strict code of behavior mirrored the boxer's spartan training. Ministers dictated when Cassius prayed, what he ate, and how he spent his leisure time. Angelo Dundee gave Cassius a rigorous routine in boxing, too: He had to be up early in the morning, eat, train, and be in bed—all according to schedule. Being a boxer and a member of the Nation of Islam required hard work, restraint, and proper nutrition, but Cassius valued all the rewards.

He decided he would live in both worlds. It was something he'd done before as an Olympic athlete and a Black man. But this time, he got to choose two spheres where he felt comfortable: Muhammad's Temple No. 29 and Dundee's 5th Street Gym. One strengthened him physically, and the other nurtured him spiritually. Cassius was careful to keep his two passions separate. No one could predict what would happen when those worlds collided.

CHAPTER TWO

THE RISE OF MALCOLM X

He spoke like a poor man and walked like a king.

—Comedian and civil rights activist Dick Gregory

On a cold April evening in 1957, Harlem was buzzing with action. Just a few hours before, cops had beaten a Black man and stuffed his limp body into a police car. Black and brown faces gathered at the scene, wondering what had happened. Some people recognized the victim who was taken by the police. Soon, accounts of the attack reached the Nation of Islam leaders. The man who was beaten was Johnson Hinton, or Johnson X, as he was known to his Muslim brothers.

Known for its rich culture, entertainment, and arts, Harlem is a historically Black neighborhood in Manhattan. Just a few years prior to this event, it was home to some of the brightest Black talents in the nation. Writers such as Zora Neale Hurston, James Baldwin, and Langston Hughes called Harlem home during the 1920s and '30s, a period known as the Harlem Renaissance. This was a time of great progress for Black artists. Harlem attracted Black creatives from across the country and promised to provide a safe and nurturing community of like-minded Black cultural leaders. It was also home to one of the largest chapters of the Nation of Islam. In Harlem, the Nation's members often preached on street corners about a better way for Black people. They weren't afraid to speak up, criticizing police who harassed the neighborhood. So, when witnesses saw Johnson X taken by police, they knew exactly what organization to go to for help.

Almost immediately, the Nation mobilized more than fifty men to go to the police precinct. The men weren't just ordinary followers but members of the Fruit of Islam, the Nation's security team of trained soldiers. They were skilled fighters who practiced boxing, judo, and more. The Fruit of Islam were forbidden from carrying weapons, but they raised fear wherever they went. This elite group of highly disciplined men was responsible for enforcing the Nation's laws and protecting its followers.

When the police looked outside the precinct on 123rd Street, they were stunned. Nearly two thousand Black people had gathered in front of the station. The members of the Nation of Islam stood in the front of the crowd with large, long coats to combat the cold. The police were afraid that the men had guns under their heavy coats. Before they could react, a tall, light-brown-skinned man with black-rimmed glasses marched into the station. It was Minister Malcolm X. He was bold, brave, and calm, and he immediately asked to see Johnson X. The police didn't know what to make of a Black man speaking with authority. At first, they told him Johnson X wasn't there, but as the crowd began to build outside, they allowed Malcolm to visit his cell. Johnson was lying on the cold jail floor, barely able to speak, visibly suffering from his head injuries. Malcolm demanded that they take him to the hospital. The lieutenant on duty was afraid that the crowd outside would riot if he didn't meet Malcolm's demands, so they called for an ambulance. Malcolm then walked out of the precinct and directed his Muslim brethren to follow him to the hospital.

Outside the Nation of Islam, very few people in the gathered crowd knew much about Malcolm. But the way he commanded the group—and how he challenged the white police officers—made everyone take notice. By the time the crowd arrived at the hospital, the doctors had treated Johnson but quicky released him, and he was shockingly taken back to jail. The crowd wanted answers and they were not going to give up. They marched right back to the precinct.

Within an hour, more than four thousand people stood in solidarity with the Nation of Islam outside the precinct. The Fruit of Islam, the skilled security team, stared straight ahead, arms crossed, waiting on orders from Minister Malcolm X. Inside the station, Malcolm negotiated with the police. There were two other Muslim men arrested with Johnson, and he made sure they were released. But the police refused to send the injured prisoner back to the hospital, insisting that he stay in jail overnight to appear in court the next morning. By 2:30 AM, officers were getting nervous about the persistent protesters. The police pleaded for Malcolm to break up the crowd, promising that Johnson would receive medical care.

Malcolm didn't want any violence. His priority was to

protect his followers. He walked outside, turned to one of his lieutenants, and whispered in his ear. Then he raised his fist, signaling for his followers to disperse. Without a word, the crowd began to leave the area. The police were stunned. They had never witnessed anyone control a crowd the way Malcolm X had that night. Reporters were shocked, too—a Black man exerting his authority over the police? *Who was this person?* they all wondered. An officer commented to a local reporter, "No one man should have that much power."

Overnight, Malcolm X and the Nation of Islam had risen to even greater status in Harlem. The Black community saw Malcolm as a hero. They were tired of police violence and eager to fight back but were unsure how. Most Black people never dared question a white man in uniform. Seeing Malcolm walk into the precinct and make demands with such confidence was inspiring. Black men, women, and children couldn't stop talking about how the Nation of Islam stood up to the police. Many of them were curious what all the fuss was about; they wanted to hear Minister Malcolm speak.

Malcolm had many followers, but his show of power in front of the police station attracted new guests to the Nation's quarters. Visitors walked up the creaking stairs of Muhammad's Temple No. 7. There, they'd see women dressed in white floor-length gowns and wearing head coverings, simple folding chairs set up for the lecture, a red Muslim flag with a white crescent moon and star, and empowering words such as *freedom* and *justice* on the wall.

At the start of every lecture, the congregation was greeted in Arabic: "As-salaam-alaikum," which means "Peace be unto you." The visitors responded in unison, "Wa-alaikum-salaam," meaning, "Peace also be unto you." Malcolm X would lecture on a variety of topics, all centering on Black Power. He spoke plainly, with language that everyone in the audience understood, delivering his message with confidence. He wanted Black people to believe in themselves and to know the truth about their history. This message offered Black audience members something different, something to be proud of.

Once new arrivals decided to join the Nation, they were called true believers. They received a different surname to mark their new identity. All members of the Nation accepted an X in place of their existing last names, which were names belonging to the white persons who had owned their ancestors. They called those last names "slave names." The X symbolized the way slavery had erased true Black identity. It was also a temporary replacement until the Messenger, Elijah Muhammad, gave the follower an Arabic last name, their "original name," such as Ali, Muhammad, Sharrieff, or Shabazz, though many of the Nation's members went years without replacing the X. Once a Muslim, you were expected to reject your slave name and break away from the past. Many Black people were eager for a different narrative, a new beginning.

Before the Johnson X incident, Malcolm's New York temple had a few hundred members. Afterward, several thousand people joined. While Malcolm's popularity grew, so did interest from the local police and FBI. The New York City police quickly became suspicious of the Nation of Islam. They sent undercover agents to spy on members and visitors of the temple. They sat in parked cars monitoring who went in and took pictures of people who came out. The police especially sought more information about "Mr. X."

The FBI was also concerned about Malcolm and his followers. They designated him a "key figure," meaning the federal government saw Malcolm X as a threat. The FBI didn't like that a Black man should lead such an effective, growing organization. They also didn't like his message of Black Power. For the rest of Malcolm's life, government agents would track his movements, document his speeches, and record his private phone calls.

This didn't stop Malcolm. He stood on street corners, outside churches, and climbed on ladders to share Elijah Muhammad's message to the public and cultivate followers. He went to places that were dangerous and communed with local criminals. Where some saw a delinquent, Malcolm saw a person who reminded him of his younger self. Where others saw an uneducated man, Malcolm saw an opportunity to speak directly, and from the heart. He understood people's frustration and shared their experiences with turmoil. Malcolm freely opened up about how Elijah Muhammad and the Nation of Islam had saved him. Anyone who listened to the charismatic minister knew about his path to a new life, but the journey that led Malcolm to the Nation had many bumps along the way.

Malcolm Little grew up in fear of what would happen next. When he was only four years old, living in Lansing, Michigan, angry white neighbors set his house on fire because they did not think his family belonged. No firefighters came to rescue them or save their burning house. It was a traumatic event that Malcolm and his siblings would relive for the rest of their lives. Malcolm's brother Wilfred remembered:

> We heard a big boom. When we woke up, fire was everywhere, and everybody was running into the walls and into each other, trying to get away. I could hear my mother yelling, my father yelling—they made sure they got us all rounded up and got us out.

Two years after that event, Malcolm's father, an outspoken Black minister, was found dead under a streetcar. During his childhood, Malcolm suspected that white supremacists killed his dad, though he never knew for certain. One of his most vivid childhood memories was the piercing sound of his mother wailing at his father's funeral. Raised fatherless, while hearing stories that white supremacists murdered his dad for challenging the social order, Malcolm grew up embittered. Years later when he was a famous spokesman for the Nation of Islam, preaching about the violent history of America, he often told white journalists, "Your father isn't here to pay his debts. My father isn't here to collect. But I'm here to collect, and you're here to pay."

After his father's death, Malcolm's mother, Louise, struggled with her mental health. She was eventually sent to a psychiatric hospital. The family was split up and Malcolm bounced around different foster homes. He was often the only Black kid at school or in his foster homes and was painfully bullied. Nearing his sixteenth birthday, Malcolm departed Lansing, Michigan, for Boston to live with his older sister, Ella.

Boston was much different from his midwestern hometown. It was a big city, with lots of opportunities to get into trouble. Malcolm quickly mixed into a rough crowd. From Boston, he eventually made his way to Harlem and became known as "Detroit Red," a moniker evoking his colorful suits and slicked-down red hair. By then Malcolm was a known thief. In 1946, he and his partners got arrested for burglary. Twenty-year-old Malcolm was transferred from prison to prison throughout Massachusetts and eventually received a letter from his brother Philbert. He explained that he and other members of the family had converted to "the natural religion for the black man": Islam.

Malcolm's siblings began writing him more frequently, educating him about Elijah Muhammad and the movement they claimed was "designed to help black people." Malcolm was interested. His father had been a reverend, a standing that aligned with his Christian upbringing, but Malcolm was searching for more—something to help him make sense of all the trauma he had gone through. He wondered what kind of new religion could give his brothers and sisters so much hope for a brighter day.

Malcolm's brother Reginald visited him in prison. He told Malcolm that there was a man who knew everything, explaining that "God is a man. His real name is Allah." Reginald said that Allah had come to America and taught everything he knew to his disciple, Elijah, "a black man just like us." Allah had instructed Elijah that the devil was also a man—the white man.

Malcolm considered this worldview. He thought about the white people he believed had killed his father, the white doctors who said that his mother was not mentally able to care for her children, the social workers who had separated his family, and the kids at the foster homes and schools who bullied him because he was Black. All of them were white and all of them were hurtful. Maybe Elijah Muhammad was right.

On August 7, 1952, Malcolm was released from prison as a new man. He was no longer Detroit Red. His commitment now was to Elijah Muhammad, and his service to the faith began as an assistant minister for the Detroit

Temple. Malcolm quickly became known as a great organizer and speaker. Muhammad sent him to Boston and then Philadelphia to build the movement. In every environment, Malcolm succeeded. He proved that he was a leader capable of bringing in new members. He was known for building trust with people. Muhammad realized that Malcolm could reach the people who were down on their luck, uneducated, or living a criminal life. He appointed Malcolm as minister of the New York City Temple No. 7, a role Malcolm took very seriously. He quickly became the most important symbol of the movement for Black Power in Black neighborhoods across northern cities. Just seven years after Malcolm was released from prison, the number of NOI (Nation of Islam) temples increased from ten to thirty. "I thank Allah for my Brother Minister Malcolm," Elijah Muhammad proudly declared.

Though Malcolm was gaining in popularity, he was still not well known across the entire country. That changed when the documentary *The Hate That Hate Produced* was televised in 1959. A New York journalist and a news anchor saw the rising popularity of the Black Muslims—as they were called by outsiders—in Harlem, and the controversy surrounding their beliefs. The two reporters decided to make a documentary about the movement. The documentary portrayed Black Muslims as adversaries of the peaceful Black civil rights leaders. The documentarians characterized the Nation of Islam as a form of "Black racism" that was "anti-white" and "anti-American," and the country responded with outrage. The Nation of Islam came under attack, and it fought back by having its star minister, Malcolm, do even more public speaking. For the next three years, Malcolm visited college campuses and delivered lectures across the country. He appeared on radio and television shows, even engaging in public debates. Malcolm X debated in the same way Cassius Clay fought, swinging from the opening bell, hitting his opponent with hard hooks and fierce jabs. He cultivated a combative style of speech, bobbing and weaving, pivoting the conversation in the direction that he wanted.

For many people, Malcolm X *was* the Nation of Islam. Some of his Muslim brothers didn't like that Malcolm was the center of attention. He was spending less time at the temple and more time traveling and speaking about politics. His topics started to deviate away from Muslim beliefs. Elijah Muhammad was watching, vigilant and newly distrustful.

To make matters worse, some of the followers closest

to Elijah spread a rumor that Malcolm wanted to take over the Nation. Elijah began to agree with their suspicions. The supreme minister didn't want Malcolm to lead the Muslims into the front lines of protests. He stressed that Black Muslims should not participate in demonstrations of any kind, fearful that such protests would incite arrests from the police or the FBI. He had even forbidden members from voting, reminding his followers that voting meant embracing a government system that would never protect the rights of Black people.

The more popular Malcolm X became, the more the government scrutinized Elijah Muhammad. On February 15, 1962, the Nation's leader wrote to Malcolm and told him not to talk about politics or civil rights anymore. The Messenger instructed the minister to stick to his teachings. A letter from Elijah Muhammad was never just a suggestion—it was a direct order.

Malcolm was loyal to Elijah, whom he credited with saving him from a life of crime. He knew he had to obey his orders but also thought the Nation should be more involved in current events affecting Black people across America. After all, there was a growing civil rights movement in the South. Civil rights leaders such as Bayard Rustin, Martin Luther King Jr., and John Lewis supported nonviolent direct action against segregation. They marched and led protests and sit-ins in segregated establishments. These leaders faced everyday threats of violence while fighting for freedom. The southern civil rights leaders had inspired a generation of young Black people to fight for change, and they demanded that America pay attention.

The Nation of Islam was strictly opposed to participating in protests and political life. Elijah saw no lasting value in integration or the expansion of civil rights. The Nation believed that Black and white people should be separate, and that no one should force them to work or live together. Their beliefs were often criticized by those who supported equality. Bayard Rustin and Malcolm X frequently faced off in debates about how best to champion the cause of Black liberation, but neither could change the other's mind. Elijah thought that the Civil Rights Movement was nothing but political performance and did not want his followers involved. And Malcolm preached what Elijah believed.

Soon Malcolm X was put to the test. Less than a month after Muhammad's order to refrain from political discourse, he had a debate with James Farmer, leader of the Congress of Racial Equality (CORE). Farmer attacked the

Nation of Islam's stance on remaining silent on issues surrounding the Civil Rights Movement. He thought that the Nation should take more action. Although Malcolm and other leaders had lots of negative things to say about white people, Farmer did not think they had any real solutions.

He directly asked Malcolm what the Nation of Islam planned to do to combat the structures of racism. To answer the question, Malcolm would have to disobey Elijah's order. He would have to take a political stance. On a national stage at Cornell University, Malcolm slowly rose from his seat and took the microphone. He seemed to search for an answer, words that would empower Black people without offending his leader. For the first time, Malcolm X wasn't the fearless voice people knew. He could not freely speak his true feelings, not about politics and the state of all Black Americans, as long as Elijah Muhammad was listening.

CHAPTER THREE

THERE'S ONLY ONE CASSIUS CLAY

Who made me is *me*.

—*Cassius Clay*

Cassius Clay was already known for his sharp tongue and showmanship when he crossed paths with another notorious athlete who encouraged him to take trash talking to the next level. On a trip to Las Vegas in June 1961, Clay met George Wagner, the most famous professional wrestler in America, while they were both in town to fight in big matches. The boxer and the wrestler were scheduled to promote their respective showdowns during the same radio broadcast.

The show's host first asked Cassius about his upcoming fight. He was facing a six-foot-seven, experienced fighter named Kolo "Duke" Sabedong. Sabedong's height and reputation made it difficult for Cassius to imagine this would be an easy win. Cassius didn't brag too much about how he would handle Sabedong, but he was confident. The host then asked the wrestler about his fight. Wagner was no stranger to the spotlight. He was one of the first to craft a sensationalized wrestling persona. Early in his career, he decided that he would play a character while wrestling. He created "Gorgeous George," a flamboyant wrestler who was known for his gold-plated hair accessories, satin outfits, sweet-smelling cologne in the ring, and villainous trash talk. Once the bell rang, Gorgeous George could do any ruthless trick or underhanded move to win a wrestling match. George was an expert showman, and he had a thing or two to teach the rising star sitting next to him.

When the host asked George to predict the outcome of his fight, he did not hold back: "I'll tear off his arm," Cassius recalled George saying. "If [he] beats me, I'll crawl across the ring and cut off my hair, but it's not gonna happen because I'm the greatest wrestler in the world."

Cassius was spellbound, remembering, "All this time,

I was saying to myself, 'Man, I want to see this fight.... I want to be there to see what happens." He loved how George hyped the action and himself. At the match a few days later, George did not disappoint. He made a grand entrance, keeping the attention of everyone who watched. George had created a character that made the fight cinematic. As Gorgeous George, he generated more interest from the media and wrestling fans. His larger-than-life persona brought hundreds of people to the matches. Cassius took notes. He told Dundee about what he saw and how he planned to improve his showmanship accordingly. Before Dundee could respond, Cassius was already committed, "This is a gooooood idea."

Leading up to his own fight in Las Vegas, Cassius told sportswriters that there was no way he could lose. He even made public predictions about which round he would knock out Sabeong: "Someone's got to go before the tenth—and you can bet it won't be me." And, just as Cassius had declared, he won the fight.

Cassius was the faster, better boxer, but Sabedong put up a serious battle. He struck him low, used his head as a third fist, and snuck in hits after the bell, when all fighting was supposed to be over. Nonetheless, Cassius had another win under his belt and a new bag of verbal tricks.

He had perfected his act, and folks were talking. Cassius even garnered several headlining nicknames: the Mighty Mouth, the Marvelous Mouth, Cash the Brash, and the famous Louisville Lip. Cassius had successfully popularized his performance persona, just as Gorgeous George had. He had learned that all of it—boxing, wrestling—was just a show. People wanted entertainment and reporters were more interested in a good story than the truth. George Wagner had taught Cassius Clay that people would pay money just to see someone shut his big mouth. He advised him to keep bragging and keep being outrageous. After just one meeting with George, Cassius became the most vocal athlete in the country.

Cassius was on a mission to make sure America knew his name. He'd begun wearing white T-shirts with CAS-SIUS CLAY printed on the front in bold red letters a few months after he arrived in Miami. The lettering style was like an old Coca-Cola logo—a very intentional design choice, since Cassius also considered himself a brand. He exercised, ate, and slept in the shirts, slowly but surely making a name for himself beyond the smaller boxing arenas and sports magazines.

Cassius wanted to be a household name. He specifically wanted to be in *Life* magazine. *Life* was popular among families across America. It was known for dazzling and creative photos that were deemed the best in the industry. Many celebrities had been featured in the publication, which at the time was considered a national favorite. If you wanted to be famous, *Life* magazine was the perfect place to start.

In September 1961, Cassius met with Flip Schulke, a photographer from *Sports Illustrated* who was assigned to take pictures of Cassius for the magazine. He followed Cassius around, snapping photos of him working out in the 5th Street Gym. During lunch together, Cassius expressed his desire to become more famous. He didn't just want to appear in sports pictures, and asked Flip for advice on how to get into *Life* magazine. Flip had recently worked on a series of underwater photos for *Life*. He wasn't sure how Cassius would fit into a family magazine. Cassius was an up-and-coming boxer who had not yet had a fight aired on national TV. He listened to the photographer's concerns, but he had his own plans. Cassius was used to promoting himself and causing a stir. This time would be no different.

The next day, Flip came to the Sir John Hotel, the boxer's home base, where he and Cassius spent time by the pool. Cassius jumped in and started doing boxing moves in the water. He splashed around, throwing punches left and right. Flip was amazed. He asked Cassius what kind of exercise he was doing. He wondered if it had anything to do with training. Cassius saw an opportunity. He told Flip that underwater workouts were part of his training. They increased his hand speed and made his punches more powerful. Flip was excited—he had never heard of anything like it. He knew this could be a great photo opportunity.

In reality, Cassius was just punching and splashing around in the water, but he made those moves look so cool and gave Flip such an interesting story that the photographer bought it. The next morning, Flip came by the hotel with an underwater camera and scuba gear. He wanted to take photos of Cassius training underwater. Cassius stood at the bottom of the pool in a flawless fighter's stance. He punched and moved as if he were in the ring. He put on a mean face for some poses and smiled for others. He was a natural model. The pictures made it into *Life* magazine just a few days later, on September 8, 1961.

This was a major victory for Cassius in shaping his public image. He was determined to become a household name and was on the fast track to making it happen. He worked hard to define how America perceived him. But as Cassius kept winning boxing matches, he began to feel that his career wasn't growing fast enough. It was time to make some new moves and reinvent himself. He knew it was time for the big league.

It had now been a year since Cassius began training with Angelo Dundee in Miami. Outside the world of boxing, the United States was growing even more tense as civil rights leaders pushed harder for equality. Inside the ring, Cassius had grown more aggressive as he fought harder to become champion. He'd gained more muscle, had perfected his boxing style, and had fought several challengers. His record was a perfect 10–0—he'd never lost a fight. Dundee knew it was time for Cassius to move on to much bigger matchups. Reporters questioned whether Cassius was ready for the big time. Sure, he had a spotless record and was a media darling, but could he handle stepping into the ring with the "big boys"? The top heavyweights were in great shape and were more experienced than Cassius. No more stepping into the ring with the older, slower boxers past their prime. This time, he'd have some real competition. Never one to back down from a fight, Cassius was ready for his next challenge. He couldn't wait to be the heavyweight champion of the world.

Cassius had been featured in countless newspaper articles by now. His sponsors back home in Louisville were pleased with his progress. It was time for him to reach the next level, which included national television coverage of his fights. Dundee patiently waited to secure the perfect opportunity for his fighter. It had to be a national fight, and he hoped it would be someone challenging, but easy enough for Cassius to beat. Dundee ultimately chose Sonny Banks, a sloppy, unpredictable fighter. In the ring, no one could anticipate what he'd do next. It seemed that he'd just come out fighting, without much thought or skill.

Dundee normally wouldn't dare pick someone like Sonny, but this fight was set at the famous Madison Square Garden (MSG) in New York City. MSG was the mecca for boxers, since all the greats fought there. But by the time Cassius was ready to enter the Garden, the arena was far from its glory days. In the 1960s, boxing had become less popular, and fights just didn't fill the seats as they used to. Even the neighborhood around the arena had deteriorated, becoming home to many fleabag hotels and fraudulent pawnshops. Cassius was not bothered by the shady surroundings. He knew that he could fill the venue's seats. He was determined to bring back the Garden's glory days and make boxing popular again.

At a crowded Boxing Writers Association of America luncheon in the winter of 1962, Clay boasted that he would save his sport the way Joe Louis once did during the Great Depression. He told everyone in attendance that he was the best thing to happen to boxing and that the world would soon know his name. He even promised to beat Sonny Banks, and proclaimed that if he didn't win, he'd take the first plane out of the country!

Not only was Cassius here to stay, he was here to become the greatest. Smiling brightly, Cassius used his sharp tongue to win over his toughest critics once again. They must have thought that anyone as brazenly confident as Cassius had to be able to back up what they were saying. One critic turned fan even noted that Cassius just might be the fighter who could save boxing and become the sport's new hero.

It was only fifteen degrees on the date of Cassius's fight at Madison Square Garden. Sure, it was a frosty February night outside, but the arena felt even colder because hardly anyone was in the audience. After all of

Cassius's big talk, he just didn't fill the seats. The boxers were already in the ring when the referee called them to the middle for instructions. Sonny was different from the other boxers Cassius had fought. He was just as young, tall, and heavy as Cassius. For once, Cassius was evenly matched. At the bell, Cassius glided toward his opponent like a ballet dancer, while Sonny moved toward him like a crab—sideways, with one hand extended outward like a pincer, and the other hand close to his body.

Cassius went to work. He circled Sonny, moving in and out of his reach, jabbed left and right, and all the while he never stopped talking. Cassius appeared in control. Sonny moved like an awkward bull and Cassius danced like a skilled, calm matador. Suddenly Cassius got too comfortable, and Sonny lashed out with a strong left hook. Before anyone knew what happened, Cassius was on the canvas. Sonny Banks had knocked down Cassius Clay!

Dundee was shocked. He'd never seen his fighter get knocked down before. Some of the folks sitting ringside cheered. Dundee didn't know what Cassius would do next, but by the count of two, he was back on his feet. To everyone's surprise, Cassius remained calm. He didn't charge at Sonny or lose his temper. He went back to the basics, jabbing and moving, his quick hands stinging his opponent like little bees. But Sonny got too excited. He started boxing wildly, something that Dundee had predicted might happen. Banks was totally unrestrained in the ring, and Cassius made him pay for it. Every time Sonny unleashed desperate punches, Cassius deftly punched back, all the while moving around the ring. By the end of the third round, Sonny was exhausted. As the fight progressed, Cassius remained in control. He had predicted the fight would end in the fourth, and it did. After a quick series of punches, Sonny staggered around the ring—he could not go on. The referee called the fight, naming Cassius Clay the winner.

Cassius now had his first top-ten placement. He was ranked either tenth or ninth, depending on the publication. Still, everyone had an opinion about his abilities. Some writers thought he was definitely one of the top five boxers in the country and should be ranked higher. Others didn't take him seriously at all and thought he was nothing but a loudmouthed fraud. Sportswriters debated about Cassius's future, some predicting a long career in boxing. Cassius and Dundee didn't mind the negative comments. Whatever people thought about

Cassius Clay was just fine, as long as they kept talking and his name remained in the papers.

By spring 1962, Cassius had become one of the most popular names in boxing. Now every promoter wanted to stage Cassius's fights, knowing he was an attraction that could make them a lot of money. Joe Louis, the great boxing hero, even made Cassius the headliner of a boxing showcase. He set him up to fight a veteran named George Logan, who gave up after fighting Cassius for four rounds.

After beating Logan, Cassius was even more confident and really worked to perfect his entrance. He came into the arena like a superstar. Even the reporters covering him thought he looked more like a popular singer than a boxer. Cassius fought, using his now-legendary footwork, and kept his face clear of any damage. He loved to brag about how "pretty" he was—that there had never been an athlete more handsome than him. And after every fight, reporters flocked to his dressing room, eager to get the next great one-liner from Cassius Clay.

In just two years of training with Dundee, Cassius had nearly climbed up to the top of the heavyweight division. There were no longer debates about his potential:

Cassius Marcellus Clay Jr. was the real deal. His grow-ing fandom meant people wanted to learn more about his life story and his personal beliefs. But Cassius was never one to let the world know his interior thoughts. He was always two steps ahead of every reporter and critic. Even though Cassius loved the spotlight, he kept parts of him-self out of the papers.

What was he *not* talking about? Only days before a major racial conflict in Los Angeles in April 1962, Cas-sius had still made no public remarks about the Civil Rights Movement or the racial injustice affecting Black Americans. This omission was no coincidence. At the time, one couldn't pick up a newspaper or turn on the TV without hearing about the latest protest or march. Being that Cassius was from Kentucky, many people assumed he had strong feelings about the news, or that he at least supported civil rights leaders in the South.

Yet whenever Cassius spoke in public, it was only about his skills, his looks, and his capabilities. It wasn't that he was unaware of or not interested in the lives of Black Americans; he wanted to keep his opinions to him-self. He also never alluded to his interest in the Nation of Islam; and he had good reason to keep his thoughts and interests private. He knew that, at this early stage of his career, he couldn't afford any politically charged, negative press. Cassius was careful to mention only ideas that supported Christian values, offhandedly saying, "I live by the Bible." While Cassius had grown up in a Christian household, his ideology was much different now. As Cassius began embracing the Nation of Islam, a movement most Americans believed was a hate cult, he knew that sharing that piece of himself with the world could mean the end of his boxing career.

CHAPTER FOUR

MUHAMMAD SPEAKS

I hope Allah will keep you wise.

—*Elijah Muhammad*

In the early 1960s, the Civil Rights Movement intensified every day. Black and white Americans everywhere clashed on the topic of racial integration. In the South, Black people pushed for immediate change—and were consistently met with violence. The world watched as Black protesters were beaten down, hosed with water, and even attacked by dogs during peaceful demonstrations. Malcolm X was also watching.

The minister was eager to join the protesters but had

been sternly warned not to get involved in what Elijah Muhammad called "politics." Malcolm still spoke out, "An eye for an eye. A tooth for a tooth. A head for a head and a life for a life. If this is the price of freedom, we won't hesitate to pay the price." Malcolm sent out a warning that anyone who touched the Black Muslims would be punished. Meanwhile, Christian leaders such as Reverend Martin Luther King Jr. preached equal rights by way of nonviolence and advised their followers never to retaliate physically against their oppressors.

In April 1962, the time finally came for Black Muslims to fight back. In Los Angeles, relationships between the police department and the Black community were strained. On April 27, two Black men were standing outside near a Nation of Islam mosque when white police officers stopped to search them. Soon, a crowd of Black Muslims came outside to see what was going on. They did not approve of the police stopping to frisk the men. The crowd continued to grow, and in a matter of minutes, shots were fired. Squad cars of backup officers rushed to the scene, and policemen raided the mosque while beating a few Black civilians with nightsticks. When the gun smoke cleared, one Nation of Islam member, Ronald Stokes, was dead, another member was paralyzed, and five others were wounded. Fourteen other Black men were placed in jail. The next morning, the *Los Angeles Times* printed a shocking headline: "'Muslims' Riot: Cultist Killed, Policeman Shot." The *New York Times* described the chaos as a "blazing gunfight," akin to a combat scene from an old western movie. And published beneath the discriminatory headlines was a disturbing picture of Ronald Stokes, handcuffed while lying lifeless on the ground.

When Malcolm heard the news, he was devastated. He knew Ronald Stokes as the secretary of the Los Angeles mosque. They had been friends for two years. He cried for his friend, but his grief quickly turned to rage. He wanted revenge. He told his assistant ministers that he planned to organize vigilantes. Before he could take any form of action, Elijah Muhammad ordered Malcolm X to stand down, saying, "Brother, you don't go to war over a provocation. They could kill a few of my followers but I'm not going to go out and do something silly." Muhammad even went as far as sending one of his top security officers to Los Angeles to make sure that no one would seek revenge against the police.

Malcolm faced an impossible decision. He knew he had to follow Elijah Muhammad's orders, but Ronald was his friend. How could he let his death go unpunished? Without approval to retaliate against the police in Los Angeles, Malcolm instead took to the podium. He knew his words had power, and he had a lot to say about what had happened to his fellow Muslim brothers in Los Angeles.

On May 4, 1962, a week after the shooting, Malcolm called a press conference in Los Angeles to stand against the police violence. By that time, six other men had died from their injuries. An investigation had also revealed that all the bullets fired by the policemen had hit the victims in their backs—except one. Which meant that the civilians had their backs turned away from the police when they were shot—they were not in any position to attack.

Malcolm boldly cried out that seven innocent men were dead because of the Los Angeles Police Department. He proclaimed the officers to be murderers. He also denounced the police chief, who had a history of using hate speech against Black people. Malcolm argued that the police chief filled his division with hatred toward the Black community they were sworn to protect. He also accused him of spreading lies about the Black Muslims, so that the public would see them as a violent group.

Malcolm did not hold back. He wanted every listener to know what the LAPD was responsible for.

The next morning, Malcolm spoke at Ronald Stokes's funeral, where more than two thousand people packed the halls of the mosque. Outside, hundreds more lined both sides of the street. The Black community had come to say goodbye to a fallen friend. At the service, some men whispered that something should be done. They complained about Elijah Muhammad's warning against revenge. Others were so angry that they decided that Muhammad was not worth their devotion, after all. They split from the Los Angeles mosque altogether. The dissidents felt they could never be free if they couldn't defend themselves.

Elijah Muhammad heard the complaints. He had eyes and ears in every city where his temples were located. He announced to his followers that it was now time to "begin the war with the [white] devil." But it wasn't the kind of war the Nation's members expected. Elijah Muhammad directed them to fight by selling newspapers. He explained that the Nation of Islam's paper, *Muhammad Speaks*, would expose white men for their crimes.

The followers could not believe the Messenger's order. Selling newspapers? The police had killed some of their own, and they were expected to fight back like this? Malcolm agreed: Selling newspapers would do nothing to confront the issue head-on. Once again, Malcolm was hurt and angry. He was even angrier when an all-white jury took only thirty minutes to rule that the LAPD was innocent of murdering the men. The entire Black community was devastated and angry, too. This was another tragedy in a long line of injustice. They were tired of being beaten down. They wanted to confront the police, even if it meant the possibility of more violence. Malcolm listened to all Black voices, Muslim and non-Muslim, on this issue. Surely, there was something else the Nation could do. Once the newspapers hit the newsstands, Malcolm realized that Elijah Muhammad was intent on staying out of the fight, even when it concerned his own devotees.

Now Malcolm X looked like a hypocrite. He had preached that the Nation of Islam was strong and would fight back. He had even warned they would not turn the other cheek if provoked. As the Black community waited for the Nation to lead the charge against the police, they questioned if all that tough talk was just for show. Their members were attacked, but the Nation of Islam just sat and waited. People in the South had been beaten and abused during protests and the Black Nationalists had no reaction.

The Ronald Stokes case elevated Malcolm to the role of national political leader. He wanted to serve as a voice for the larger Black community, not just the Nation of Islam. He preached less about Elijah Muhammad's religious teachings and focused instead on current events. What happened in Los Angeles had deepened Malcolm's internal conflict with the Nation. He respected Elijah Muhammad, but he knew that expressing his political convictions was just as important as his faith. Malcolm wanted the Nation to get involved in the larger struggle—equal rights and justice for all Black people. He began to understand that working together was more important than who was right or wrong. Malcolm soon called for Black unity, beyond the constraints of religion. He urged Black Americans to come together "against the common enemy." As Malcolm began meeting with civil rights leaders, Elijah Muhammad was watching.

When Muhammad heard that Malcolm had called for unity and was working with groups outside the Nation, he demanded that his minister return home to Harlem. He did not want him leading demonstrations or getting more attention from the FBI. The Nation could not afford for its prized speaker to get arrested or even killed by the police.

In truth, Elijah Muhammad was worried that he was losing control of Malcolm. FBI agents listening in on Muhammad's phone calls to his advisers learned that he had become alarmed about Malcolm X's restlessness. He worried there was no one who could "control Malcolm." Still, he called his minister and advised him to "play dead on everything." To Malcolm, this wasn't possible. How could he ignore what was going on in America? Elijah Muhammad sensed Malcolm's hesitation. Before he got off the phone, he warned, "I hope Allah will keep you wise." Malcolm didn't have to guess what that meant.

Regardless of his convictions about the fight for civil rights, Malcolm knew that he still had to follow orders. Instead of joining local protesters in Harlem, he stood across the street and watched them. Sometimes, he'd visit civil rights meetings and just sit in the back quietly. Elijah Muhammad had informers planted everywhere, and Malcolm didn't want anyone to mistake his presence for activism. The Black community was also watching, and they weren't pleased. They saw that Malcolm talked a good game but never actually did anything. The Nation of Islam no longer seemed like the heroes who had taken on the New York police on the streets of Harlem.

While the Nation of Islam tried to keep a low profile during the Civil Rights Movement, the FBI was doing its best to uncover information that could discredit the Nation for good. Soon, the bureau's agents found just what they were looking for. The Nation of Islam was founded on ideas about morality and discipline. Followers prayed at specific times, had to remain healthy, and were ordered to be faithful to their spouses. Many of the Nation's members lived in poverty but were required to give $3.30 a week—which amounts to a little over $30 today—to the organization. In some mosques, the weekly tithes were even higher. During mass meetings, participants were expected to buy copies of *Muhammad Speaks* and even give additional donations. Elijah Muhammad was the creator and the enforcer of those rules, yet he did not live by them—he frequently misused the Nation's funds for his personal life and cheated on his wife through repeated affairs with other women in the NOI.

The FBI had informants working on the inside of the Nation. These individuals pretended to be Black

Muslims and would report back to the FBI about what was going on inside. The informants revealed that Elijah Muhammad had relationships with seven women outside his marriage and had had children with each of them. The FBI also confirmed that Muhammad rode around in expensive cars and had multiple homes, while many of his low-income followers struggled to pay dues to the Nation. He even referred to the Nation's relief funds as "my checking account."

The FBI wanted to create distrust within the organization, and this was the perfect way to make followers turn away from Elijah Muhammad. They intended to spread these scandals through anonymous letters. Malcolm X, however, had already gotten the news. For years, he heard rumblings that Elijah Muhammad was not the man he presented to the public. Ever loyal, Malcolm dismissed the rumors. But the alarming accounts persisted, from Chicago to New York.

By 1962, Malcolm noticed that many Muslim followers were losing their faith and leaving the cause. The minister was distraught and had nightmares about the end of the Nation of Islam. He thought that journalists would eventually confront him about Elijah Muhammad's lies. Finally, Malcolm accepted the harsh truth that Elijah

Muhammad had betrayed the Nation. Malcolm was disappointed in his leader. He was even more disappointed that Elijah Muhammad would not admit to his wrongs. Malcolm's disappointment led to doubt, which in turn sent Malcolm down a dangerous path of questioning everything Elijah Muhammad had ever taught him.

In contrast to Elijah's extravagant life, Malcolm X and his wife, Betty, lived on a strict budget. They owned almost nothing, not even their home. Because Malcolm was the voice of the Nation of Islam, many outsiders believed he had money. Even some of the Black Muslims assumed that Malcolm had access to a lot of money—that's what they wanted to believe, anyway. The minister's enemies were eager to pin down any kind of wrongdoing. Malcolm, on the other hand, was not so much concerned about the politics of the Nation of Islam's leadership as he was focused on the struggle for Black freedom.

At a Harlem rally on May 26, 1962, he suggested that local civil rights leaders coordinate a movement against police brutality. His message would reach listeners all the way to California. One month later, during a press conference, the Los Angeles mayor played an informant's recording of Malcolm speaking at a Muslim gathering. Malcolm had laughed in response to a recent international plane crash that killed one hundred white American passengers. He told his followers that Allah had answered his prayers by destroying the plane. America was stunned. Malcolm's comments supported what many had feared—that he was a violent man determined to spread a message of hate. In Atlanta, Reverend Martin Luther King Jr. denounced Malcolm's comments. He didn't believe that any race—any group—should delight in another's pain. King spread a message of unity and integration. The Nation of Islam, and by extension Malcolm X, spread the message that Black people should thrive together, without white people. In response, King gave a powerful warning, "Black supremacy is as dangerous as white supremacy."

At this point, Malcolm faced more criticism than ever, and he hid from the spotlight accordingly. He declined interview requests from radio programs and television shows. Facing a firestorm of attacks, Malcolm traveled to Detroit, where Elijah Muhammad was scheduled to deliver a major address on June 10 at Olympia Stadium. As the minister avoided the public eye, he was about to meet someone who loved to live in the spotlight.

That same day in Michigan, before the rally was scheduled to begin, Cassius Clay and his brother, Rudy, visited a diner filled with Black customers, and there they met Malcolm. Cassius introduced himself, assuming Malcolm had heard of him before, but the minister didn't know the boxer. Malcolm did not read about boxing in newspapers or watch fights on television. Although they spoke only briefly, Malcolm instantly knew that there was something special about the young man.

Moments before the rally inside Olympia Stadium began, Cassius entered the building, ushered into a long line of Black spectators who were escorted to their seats on the right side of the floor. All the men wore dark suits, and all the women, seated on the left, were dressed in beautiful white gowns and shawls. When Malcolm X took the stage, Cassius listened intently as the minister delivered the Nation's doctrine: "We are not a sect or a cult, nor are we a hate group. We are a group of people who have accepted the Islamic faith and believe that Allah is the Supreme Being."

After Malcolm spoke, Elijah Muhammad took the stage. He was a frail man, having suffered from severe asthma for most of his adult life. Elijah often had coughing spells while he talked. He wasn't a particularly exciting speaker, but his leadership position made people respect his words. For two hours, he preached about Black communities separating from white Americans. The Clay brothers applauded his message. Being able to see Elijah Muhammad in person meant the world to Cassius. That day in Detroit changed his life and brought him closer to the Nation of Islam.

A few months later, in mid-August, Cassius Clay showed up for another Nation of Islam rally in St. Louis. Dressed like the other men in the Nation, wearing a dark suit, white shirt, and bow tie, Cassius smiled for a photographer from *Muhammad Speaks*—the Black Muslims' newspaper. He seemed completely comfortable posing for the camera with his brother and a group of Black men, as if someone was snapping a picture of him at a family reunion instead of a Nation of Islam meeting. No one interviewed him for *Muhammad Speaks*, as athletes received little coverage in the newspaper at that time. He was not yet considered an important figure in Elijah Muhammad's agenda, but this was the second time in two months he had traveled a great distance to hear the Messenger speak and to see Malcolm again.

Despite the risks of being associated with the Nation of Islam, Cassius could not stay away. At a time when the

FBI was conducting an extensive investigation into the Black Muslims, Cassius Clay put his entire career in danger by engaging with Elijah Muhammad and Malcolm X. But like so many people who heard Malcolm speak, Cassius was mesmerized by the minister's brilliance: the way he told stories using his great intellect and flashes of humor. The more Cassius listened to Malcolm, the deeper he fell under his influence. Over the next year, Cassius's fascination with Malcolm and the Nation evolved alongside his growing fame as a boxer and he developed a secret friendship with the minister. In the summer of 1962, the charismatic minister had sparked something in Cassius. Neither man knew it then, but Malcolm would play a major role in the young boxer's life.

CHAPTER FIVE

ALLAH APPROVES

It's heresy to imply that I am in any way
whatever even equal to Mr. Muhammad.
No man on earth today is his equal.

—*Malcolm X*

In early 1963, while Cassius Clay was riding a wave of boxing wins and growing popularity, Malcolm X faced new challenges within the Nation of Islam. Elijah Muhammad was in poor health. He had a persistent asthmatic cough and was forced to cancel several public appearances. Muhammad's children worried about the fate of the organization. If something happened to their father, who would be in charge?

They had heard whispers that Malcolm X was aspiring to inherit their father's role. He was an intelligent leader and a popular speaker. Considering his fragile condition, Elijah Muhammad had even asked the minister to preside over the annual Saviour's Day convention in Chicago, the holiest day of ceremonies for the Nation of Islam. Because of Malcolm's popularity, many considered him the Nation's spokesperson. However, Elijah Muhammad's children didn't trust Malcolm X. They did not want him to lead the convention. They would never accept him as their father's second-in-command.

Malcolm had more important problems to address. On the eve of the convention in late February 1963, he had learned of all of Elijah's marital infidelities. After Saviour's Day, Malcolm visited several of the women whose children were fathered by Elijah Muhammad. They told him that Elijah thought Malcolm was the best minister in the Nation but that his ambition made him "dangerous." The Messenger said that Malcolm wanted too much power. Malcolm was shocked to learn Elijah Muhammad's true feelings. He learned that Elijah praised him to his face but talked about him behind his back. Malcolm couldn't believe the man who had "saved his life" now betrayed him.

When Malcolm returned home to New York from Chicago, he had no idea how to handle Elijah's betrayal. But he knew he had a big prizefight to attend, and a charming young boxer to support. Malcolm planned to sit ringside at Madison Square Garden at Cassius Clay's next match. Since meeting Cassius nine months earlier, Malcolm reflected on the cultural power champions possessed. They could influence people and unite a generation. He remembered how he felt watching Joe Louis fight in the 1930s. The fighter wasn't a hero just to *him*—Joe had the support of every Black person Malcolm knew. In 1937, when Louis won the heavyweight championship—only the second Black man to ever hold the title—the country celebrated in streets, in homes, and even on the side of the road. Black people were proud of his triumph. Every Black child old enough to raise a fist wanted to be the next Joe Louis.

Malcolm realized that Cassius could be that next great Black American sports hero. He also saw that Cassius, unlike Joe Louis, refused to let anyone control him—not sponsoring groups, not fans or journalists, not even his trainer, Angelo Dundee. Cassius had shown that he was independent and freethinking. Many white boxing fans and sportswriters did not approve of his trash talking in the ring. They preferred he just stay quiet and fight. They also wanted him to be humble, like Joe Louis, but that just wasn't Cassius's style. Malcolm X saw great potential in the boxer: he spoke his mind, attended Muslim meetings, and sought Malcolm's mentorship. Most important, Cassius risked his career by associating with a divisive organization such as the Nation of Islam. To Malcolm, that proved he could be trusted.

And while Malcolm saw the potential in Cassius, Cassius found a spiritual and political role model in Malcolm. Cassius had attended more Black Nationalist meetings since his first encounter with the minister. He had even memorized some of Elijah's and Malcolm's speeches. Cassius was bursting with knowledge and new purpose. However, he wasn't ready to reveal to the world his allegiance to the Nation. He knew he could be a powerful voice to carry Elijah Muhammad's message, but first he needed to fulfill his own dreams. He needed to become the heavyweight champion.

On March 13, 1963, Cassius Clay was scheduled to box the third-ranked heavyweight contender, Doug Jones, at Madison Square Garden in New York City. The Louisville Lip could pull in the crowd, while Doug was boring in comparison. Outside the ring, he didn't have much personality. Still, both boxers did their best to promote the fight. They had a little over a month to get people interested and fill seats. Cassius's first promotional stop was *The Ed Sullivan Show*, a popular television program. There, he wowed the crowd with his rhyming predictions and charm.

"Suppose I were to box you, how far would I go?" Sullivan asked.

"Well, Ed, if you run, I'll have to cut it to one."

"One round?"

"No, one punch."

Cassius even did a magic trick. He was a magician in and out of the ring, and to prove his point, he took a blue scarf out of his pocket, waved it a few times, then *poof!* The scarf transformed into a cane. The audience loved it.

A few days later, Cassius worked to impress a much different crowd. He traveled to Albany, where a joint legislative committee was having a hearing about the future of boxing in New York State. Boxers, journalists, and even baseball players showed up to support the boxing community. They wanted to convince lawmakers not to ban organized boxing forever. Boxing is safer than baseball, judged Gil McDougald, a former New York Yankees infielder. James L. Hicks, a Black journalist, testified that boxing "is one area of the sports world where equal opportunity is granted to members of my race."

Dressed in a dark suit and bow tie, Cassius Clay stood up to speak. He compared boxing to the natural change of seasons, "In the winter, things are cold, things are dead. Spring will come again, and so will summer." Of course, Cassius considered his career to be the spring that had finally come following the long winter of boxing. Ever the showman, he also took the opportunity to promote his upcoming fight at Madison Square Garden. Cassius made a lasting impression that day.

With only a few weeks left to train before his big fight at MSG, Cassius headed to Miami to work out at the 5th Street Gym. Sonny Liston was also in town for a rematch against Floyd Patterson. Liston wasn't concerned about another fight with Patterson. He had vowed to knock him out even quicker than before.

Sonny was more concerned with Cassius and wanted to see what his future opponent was up to. When Cassius saw him at the gym, he yelled: "Get him out of here, [he] is spying on me." The boxers went back and forth, yelling insults at each other. Sonny got so mad that he charged at Cassius, but Cassius moved back through the ropes into the security of the ring before he could reach him. Sonny left angrily, but Cassius smiled. He knew he had gotten under the skin of a champion. It was a small victory, but it proved that Cassius could quickly make Sonny lose his composure. In the battle for heavyweight champion, focus and composure were key.

Back in New York City a few days later, the count-down to Madison Square Garden's big fight was on. Cassius doubled down on publicizing the event in order to sell tickets. But no one was covering his interviews. The newspaper union members had gone on strike a few weeks before. The timing couldn't have been worse. Of all the sports, the strike affected boxing the most. Unlike in baseball or football, there were no seasons in boxing, so fans checked newspapers for upcoming fights. Boxing promoters depended on sportswriters to get the word out about upcoming matches. It was the sportswriters who interviewed fighters, visited training camps, and created heroes. The news blackout was a serious problem for Cassius just days before his big fight.

Cassius had to find another outlet to generate more buzz. He quickly got back on TV, where his charm and good looks were sure to garner attention. The week before the fight, he appeared on popular programs such as *The Today Show* and *The Tonight Show*, and also returned to *The Ed Sullivan Show*. Many Americans weren't sure if Cassius Clay was a boxer or an actor. For years, pictures of beaten-down, bloody men represented the idea of a boxer. They were mostly quiet, avoiding public speaking. Cassius was funny, poised, and interesting. He was everything the typical boxer was not. Cassius even made personal appearances, just like a presidential candidate. He got onstage at poetry contests and would also share some of his writing. At one reading, he worked the crowd—pausing and adding a bit of swagger to his verse:

> *My secret is self-confidence—*
> *A champion at birth;*
> *I'm lyrical, I'm fresh, I'm smart—*
> *My fists have proved my worth*

The crowd loved him. Throughout the week, Cassius went from TV show interviews to riling up passersby on street corners—anything to promote his fight. He understood how to use the media to sell his image. He quickly figured out that becoming famous was just a matter of delivering the same message to the same people, over and over. The more he bragged, the more promoters took an interest in him. Cassius knew that his words sparked a media buzz, and a buzz created lots of money.

On the morning of March 16, 1963, Cassius was up and dressed by six thirty. He walked the two blocks from his hotel to Madison Square Garden and looked at the large marquee: TONIGHT—BOXING—CLAY VS. JONES. He looked at the smaller sign at the ticket booth that summarized his weeks-long media blitz: SOLD OUT. Sure, Cassius had sold out smaller venues in the past, but seeing this sign at the historic Madison Square Garden meant the world to him. For the first time in six years, all of the Garden's 18,732 seats were filled. It was also the first time the venue ever sold out ahead of a match. For Cassius, this was a childhood dream come true. Selling out the Garden was proof that Cassius Clay was the greatest; just as he had proclaimed.

Now it was time for the action. Cassius had predicted that Doug Jones would go down in the fourth round. With a sold-out crowd gathering outside, Cassius relaxed in his room before the match. People around the boxer were always coming and going. So he didn't think much when a Black man walked into his quarters. The man looked around at the cluttered space and locked eyes with the boxer. "Who takes care of you?" he asked.

Cassius looked up and pointed to his trainer, Dundee. The man started to give Dundee orders, telling him to polish Cassius's shoes and wash the boxer's socks.

The stranger—a man named Drew "Bundini" Brown— thought that Cassius needed to look just right for tonight's big fight. Bundini had walked uninvited into the box- er's life and decided to stay. A talent like Cassius needed someone to take care of him, and he gladly volunteered for the role. When Cassius left in a limo to go to the Garden, Bundini sat in the back seat with him. When traffic was slow, Bundini ordered the driver to drive on the sidewalk. And when the police came to ask why the limo was on the sidewalk, Bundini told them that Cassius Clay was in the car, and if it wasn't for him, "they wouldn't be out there on duty." Bundini was bold, with a larger-than-life personal- ity. And Cassius loved it.

That night, Madison Square Garden came alive once again. The match had a few notable guests. Baseball legend Jackie Robinson, tennis star Althea Gibson, and Nobel Peace Prize winner Ralph Bunche were all near the ring. Other athletes, such as Sugar Ray Robinson, and politicians, including New York State's Joint Legis- lative Committee on Professional Boxing, were there to witness the show.

Malcolm X was sitting ringside, eager to watch Cassius Clay make magic. None of the reporters covering the fight had any idea that Malcolm had begun forging a bond with the young contender. Boxing events in New York City, where the minister was based, made it possible for Cassius to meet privately with Malcolm. Looking around the Garden, Malcolm realized all the people present had come for one man: Cassius Clay. He had never seen so many people drawn to an event because of a single Black man. Not even Elijah Muhammad, he must have thought, could fill the Garden.

While many were there to support Cassius, others rooted against him. They weren't impressed with his television appearances and thought he needed to be humbled. When Cassius walked out, some in the crowd booed.

The first round began with Cassius on his toes, circling away from Doug's punches. But less than a minute into the match, Cassius made a huge mistake. He had a habit of avoiding punches by moving straight back instead of slipping left or right. Throughout his career, boxing critics had called out that bad move. This time, the error allowed Doug to lunge forward and land a hard blow on Cassius's chin. The hit was so powerful that Cassius stumbled back into the corner ropes. The punch stunned him. It was clear that he was hurt, and the shocked crowd rose out of their seats. Once Cassius cleared his head, he regained control of the fight. He boxed like a veteran, making sure to pace himself. Doug missed an opportunity to dominate the fight, and Cassius had learned valuable information: He had taken Doug's best punch and knew just how fast his opponent could strike.

The big electric clock in the Garden counted down the seconds in each round. Cassius had predicted that Doug would be defeated in just four rounds. He knew that he had to back up his words or look like a fool. In the fourth round, he quickly increased his attacks, but Doug was ready—preventing Cassius from making any big moves. And the critics were right there to savor Cassius's struggles, yelling insults his way. Cassius ended the round by landing a hard right, but it wasn't enough to secure the win. The fight continued, with the crowd cheering for Doug and booing Cassius. If you were listening to a broadcast, you'd assume that Doug was winning. That wasn't the case. Neither fighter gained an advantage during the middle rounds. Something big would have to happen for Cassius to get the upper hand and for him to silence the hecklers. In the last three rounds,

Cassius gave his all. He consistently landed three or four times as many punches as Doug. It was clear that Cassius wanted a win: He fought with heart, closing the distance between himself and Jones. The final bell rang and the boxers went to their corners. The judges now had to decide the winner. Both men thought they deserved a victory. Doug was the crowd's favorite.

The wait between the final bell and the decision was almost unbearable. Finally, by the slimmest scoring margins, the judges gave the fight to Cassius. He had won, and boos showered the ring. Spectators complained the match was unfair and threw cups and programs at him, yelling, "Fix! Fix! Fix!" Then, "Fake! Fake! Fake!"

Cassius didn't care. He raised his hands in triumph and mimicked the booing fans. He frowned his face and stuck out his tongue at the cameras. Some reporters asked if he'd fight Doug again, just to prove that he had won fairly. Cassius quickly shut down that idea. He had his eyes on a bigger name—Sonny Liston. And Liston was ready for him.

Sonny had watched the Clay-Jones fight and told reporters that Cassius needed to learn how to duck and run. He didn't think Cassius stood a chance against him. While Sonny discredited Cassius's boxing style, something else about the potential matchup piqued his interest. He saw that boxing fans would pay to see someone silence the Louisville Lip. Whether Sonny liked it or not, Cassius drew a crowd, and crowds meant big money. Liston geared up for a hefty payday.

After the fight with Doug Jones, Cassius was a true celebrity and a rich man. He now had more money than most Black youths ever dreamed of. Money allowed Cassius to live the life he'd always wanted—though it did not eliminate the evils of segregation. If a restaurant refused to serve him, he'd simply order whatever he wanted at his hotel or have his personal chef prepare a meal. To Cassius, wealth allowed him to sidestep many forms of discrimination. By the end of 1963, he'd made $81,000, which was almost as much as President John Kennedy's $100,000 annual salary. His success as a boxer earned him economic independence, the kind that Elijah Muhammad promoted. Money, Muhammad preached, gave Black men freedom. Cassius might not have talked publicly about discrimination, but he projected a more militant, defiant posture, rejecting any notion of racial inferiority. When he boldly shouted, "I am the greatest," he defined his self-worth on his own terms, expressing an emerging attitude of Black Power.

Cassius represented a new generation of Black youth who were unafraid of testing limits. Because he was so fearless, news writers began to compare him to the young Black students fighting for racial justice in the South, including James Meredith. In Mississippi, Meredith became the first Black student to integrate Ole Miss, the University of Mississippi. He faced angry mobs, who threatened his life. It was a turbulent time in America. Race divided the country and everyday heroes pushed for integration and equality. For Cassius to be compared to James Meredith meant that he, too, was ready to fight for integration, or at least that he was ready to publicly support the cause. But that couldn't be further from the truth.

Cassius had never shown an interest in politics, especially not racial integration. "I believe it's human nature to be with your own kind," he declared. "I don't want people who don't want me. I don't like people who cause trouble." The Civil Rights Movement, he said, was not like a boxing match. "There's no referee." So, when he volunteered to raise money for the NAACP, the largest

Black civil rights organization, it seemed that he had changed his mind. Many thought this was his way of entering the national conversation about race.

However, Cassius Clay ultimately made explicit his philosophy: Black people should enforce "eye-for-an-eye" retaliation against the violence committed by white supremacists. Cassius didn't believe in the nonviolent protests and marches that were being organized in the South. He went on to criticize the NAACP as ignorant for not striking back when people attacked them at protests. Cassius had always strayed away from taking a stance on racial issues, and now he found himself in the middle of a controversy.

The NAACP was a highly respected organization, and Cassius had just belittled them. Many Black people were disappointed to learn that one of the most famous Black athletes in the country didn't support integration; instead, he embraced the separatist ideology of the Nation. They began to wonder who had been influencing Cassius. Soon enough, rumors emerged about his new friends, the Black Muslims. Some of Cassius's white sponsors in Louisville were worried that he had made a terrible mistake, alienating much of the country. Cassius didn't back down. He made it clear that he was not interested in integration. He was more interested in becoming wealthy and independent—two things that he felt ensured his freedom as a Black man in America. Clearly, Malcolm's lessons were making an imprint on him. "I feel free since I learned the truth about myself and my people," he said.

As Cassius developed a more independent mindset, Malcolm hesitated, unsure of his future. He continued to worry that members of the Nation of Islam would leave the organization if they learned about Elijah Muhammad's other families. The Messenger's deceptions forced Malcolm to confront a difficult truth. For years, he had built up Elijah as an honorable man, but Malcolm no longer believed it. He had to confront Elijah about his immoral behavior. But after talking with him, Malcolm felt uneasy about holding Elijah up to the Nation as a prophet. Malcolm faced a great crisis of faith that would test his loyalty to the Messenger, and that allegiance wavered even more as the fight for civil rights spurred increasingly brutal attacks on Black people.

In the South, the struggle for integration was becoming more violent.

The Ku Klux Klan, a white supremacist hate group, bombed Martin Luther King's organizing headquarters at the A. G. Gaston Motel in Birmingham, Alabama. Many people spoke out against the hateful act and offered their support. Black celebrities such as Jackie Robinson and Floyd Patterson went to Birmingham to stand together with the peaceful protesters and organizers. Malcolm X admired the courage of Birmingham's youth, but he could not believe King would allow them to march on the front lines. Malcolm also criticized celebrities for their roles in these demonstrations, claiming that they were being used by white liberals to pacify Black protesters. He was especially critical of Jackie Robinson.

Jackie was now an older man who needed a cane to get around. He was considered a legend by most Americans. When he stepped up to speak alongside King at the Sixth Avenue Baptist Church in Birmingham, everyone clapped for him. They remembered that he was a proud, fearless Black man who had integrated Major League Baseball years earlier. Malcolm thought that Jackie was too passive, calling him a traitor for working with white politicians. He had endured many racist attacks during his time as a baseball player and, like Martin Luther King, chose a nonviolent approach.

Jackie had a few fighting words of his own for Malcolm. He stated what many others were thinking: that

Malcolm had never taken action. After all, he never went South to endorse protests; he had never stood up to the racist mobs attacking Black activists. And for all their talk about protecting the youth and women, Malcolm and the Nation of Islam had never taken steps to avenge anyone—not even when their own members were attacked by the police in Los Angeles. For Malcolm, it was a stinging criticism. Jackie Robinson didn't know that, deep down, Malcolm X wanted to participate in this movement concentrated in the South, but Elijah Muhammad had forbidden him. He had no idea that members of the Nation of Islam were ready to retaliate as soon as Elijah said the word.

Even though Malcolm had critiqued Jackie Robinson and Floyd Patterson, he understood the power Black athletes had. They exuded hope and could influence both Black and white fans. Malcolm X had influence as well, but his enormous potential for reaching a Black audience beyond the Nation had not yet been fully realized. A writer named Alex Haley found the minister more compelling than any speaker he'd ever heard. He'd interviewed him before but wanted to learn more about how Malcolm Little had become Malcolm X. He also thought Malcolm was the brains behind the Nation's success, but

Malcolm quickly corrected him, saying: "Sir, it's heresy to imply that I am in any way whatever even equal to Mr. Muhammad. No man on earth today is his equal." Haley was intrigued. He wanted to write an autobiography of Malcolm X. After considering the idea, Malcolm agreed, on two conditions: First, all his profits from the book would go directly to the Nation of Islam; second, Elijah Muhammad must approve the project. Once Alex agreed and told Malcolm that the book would help spread the Nation's message, they had a deal. The minister simply said, "Allah approves."

Malcolm didn't trust journalists, but he eventually opened up to Alex Haley in light of their collaboration on the book. The pair planned their next meeting, and Malcolm handed Alex a handwritten note. The note was a dedication: "This book I dedicate to The Honorable Elijah Muhammad, who...pulled me out, cleaned me up, and stood me on my feet, and made me the man that I am today." Haley filed away the dedication to use later. No one could imagine how much Malcolm's life would change by the time the book was complete.

CHAPTER SIX

WHEN CHICKENS COME HOME TO ROOST

I'm for the Black Muslims.

—*Cassius Clay*

Weeks after defeating Doug Jones at MSG, Cassius was still giving people something to talk about. When asked about racial integration, Cassius said that it was a bad idea, dangerous, even, for Black people. His comment was an affront to all the hard work civil rights leaders had accomplished. Reporters had a field day using Cassius's words to put a dent in his otherwise solid reputation. He had already offended the NAACP and now his sponsors were worried about their investment. They thought the boxer's relationship with the Muslims would end his career. They blamed Malcolm X for Cassius's bold statements. Almost overnight, the sponsors devised a plan to get Cassius away from nosy reporters, and far away from his Black Muslim associates. They decided to create some physical distance between Cassius Clay and Malcolm X. Cassius went off to London, where he would fight British heavyweight Henry Cooper on June 18, 1963.

As soon as he stepped foot in England, Cassius took over the headlines. He went after his opponent, calling him a bum, and dazzling the British reporters with his rhyming insults. Soon the match was underway, and Cassius put on a show...or maybe, a circus. He made a mock royal entrance to the event, wearing a tilted crown, and was preceded by British and American soldiers. The sound of trumpets and boos blasted through the stadium as Cassius smiled at his critics. The British reporters said he had gone too far, poking fun at the royal family. For Cassius, it was all a performance. He knew how to light up a crowd and he had learned a long time before to drown out the boos by paying attention to his own voice—the only voice that mattered.

Dozens of celebrities sat ringside, including Elizabeth

Taylor and Richard Burton, ready to watch the American star get knocked out in the ring. Cassius's British opponent, Henry Cooper, was a pretty good boxer with a great left hand. However, he was a bleeder—his face had so many delicate old scars that it was easy for one of them to reopen, putting him at a disadvantage in the ring. As with any match, too many cuts or too much blood meant the end of a fight, and a loss for the bleeder. Henry's goal was to win before the referee could call it when his wounds opened. It was his best chance against Cassius Clay.

Without hesitation, Henry began the fight as if he were on a mission. He lunged at Cassius, throwing long, wild punches. His efforts paid off. Soon Cassius had a cut on his nose. The crowd exploded with loud cheers. A British fighter might finally shut the Louisville Lip! However, defeating Cassius was no small feat. In the second round, Cassius opened one of Henry's old wounds with a slicing punch. By the end of the round, he'd punctured a few more wounds with his quick jabs. Henry's left eye was starting to look bad. His plan to quickly take down Cassius before he began bleeding had failed.

By that point, Cassius knew he'd won, so he took some time to put on a show. He began shouting at fans close to the ring. He even dared Henry to hit him, making a grand gesture of sticking out his chin to invite a punch! And while Cassius was having a good time playing games with his opponent, Henry saw an opening. He lunged at him and hit him square on the cheek with a heavy left hook. Cassius fell to the floor of the ring like a crumbled paper bag. The crowd roared as the bell ended the round. Dundee helped Cassius back to his corner. He couldn't believe what Henry had done! Cassius even took a while to regain his senses. It was a big victory for Henry, but his luck would not last long.

During the next round, Cassius went in for the win. He beat Henry so badly that the referee had to stop the fight. Despite his brutal hooks, Henry was no match for Cassius. Back in the locker room, Cassius told reporters that Henry wasn't a bum, after all. The boxer was humble and kind, back to being the charmer that everyone loved. The show—his fight—was over and there was no need to perform any longer. And just as quickly as he had arrived, Cassius was on a plane headed back to America. He was one more victory closer to the heavyweight title fight.

Cassius had been away for a few months and missed his friends at the mosque. If his sponsors thought that traveling to England would get Cassius to forget about the

Nation of Islam, they were sorely mistaken. When Cassius returned to the United States, he had a lot of free time. That meant he could attend more Nation of Islam gatherings. His friendship with Malcolm X grew stronger. Malcolm advised him on spiritual and professional issues. Cassius saw Malcolm as an older brother and Malcolm loved him like a little brother.

Now Cassius was going in and out of mosques so often that a journalist was bound to see him. Cassius was famous. He had been featured in magazines and appeared on top-rated television shows. He was too well known to go unrecognized in public. It was only a matter of time before reporters noticed something crystal clear: Cassius Clay was a member of the Nation of Islam.

One hot summer day in Chicago, Cassius was finally forced to address questions about his membership in the Nation of Islam. A reporter had followed him as he left an Islamic school in his red Cadillac, shouting questions between stoplights as he hung out the window of his own car. It was like a scene out of a movie. No matter how fast Rudy and Cassius drove, they couldn't get rid of the reporter. Finally, the reporter asked a direct question: "Are you a Black Muslim?" Cassius didn't answer. The boxer only worked up the courage to speak one block later. But he wasn't sure exactly how to respond. Cassius was used to putting on a show, to giving people what they wanted. This question was about his personal life. How he answered it could change the way people thought of him or, worse, it could cost him a chance at the title. If Cassius answered the question honestly, admitting he had embraced the Nation of Islam, no boxing promoter would ever offer him a shot at the heavyweight championship.

Cassius finally decided to respond. First, he said no, he was not a member of the Nation. Then he quickly changed to "I don't know," and finally he said, "I'm for the Black Muslims." Although he didn't say much, he had said enough to potentially compromise his heavyweight championship dreams.

The next day, he made sure to distance himself from the Nation. Reporters asked him to clarify rumors that he was a Black Muslim. This time, Cassius knew exactly how to handle the media. He said that he was still searching for an organization to join, but he didn't have the time or experience to lead civil rights groups. He proclaimed that he didn't belong to any organization. Soon, Cassius served up a different topic of conversation: He began boasting about taking down Sonny Liston. The reporters followed Cassius down any and every rabbit hole. He was a master at giving the media something to talk about and was careful not to let them focus on any topic that could make him vulnerable.

Malcolm X agreed, at least publicly, that Black athletes and entertainers should not define or lead the Civil Rights Movement. On July 22, 1963, the day of the Sonny Liston–Floyd Patterson rematch in Las Vegas, Malcolm's own fight was in Brooklyn, where more than a thousand protesters were demonstrating against racial discrimination at a hospital construction site. What did a million-dollar contest in Las Vegas have to do with the fight against discrimination? Robert Lipsyte, a young *New York Times* reporter, had asked. Malcolm X dismissed him: "That's a stupid question."

"The only stupid question is the unanswered question," Lipsyte replied. Smiling, Malcolm nodded to his bodyguards to let the reporter through. "I'm pleased to see that the two best men in the sport are Black," he said. "But they'll be exploited, of course, and the promoters will get all the bread." Malcolm X, the single-minded revolutionary, obviously knew something about boxing.

That same day, Sonny Liston won his rematch against Floyd Patterson. He secured his title as the heavyweight champion of the world—which, to many fans, was disappointing. Sonny's public record was stained by confrontations with the police, arrests for various crimes, and stints in prison. They wanted someone with a spotless background and good public image to beat Sonny. Cassius Clay was the clear choice. He was likable and had won over the media with his loudmouth antics and charming guy-next-door smile. Cassius was a star. He even considered himself more an entertainer than a boxer, identifying more with musicians Sam Cooke and Elvis Presley than with Sonny Liston and Floyd Patterson. And while he posed for pictures or did interviews with countless journalists, Cassius kept his true feelings to himself. He showed fans and reporters what they wanted: a nice guy who'd make you forget he was a trained fighter. He needed everyone to be charmed and occupied, so that they wouldn't pry into his personal life and beliefs. He knew he couldn't keep his secret forever, but he just needed more time. Aiming to take the heavyweight title from Sonny, Cassius knew the timing wasn't right to reveal his relationship to the Nation of Islam. However, while Cassius kept a low profile as a Black Nationalist until the right moment emerged, his mentor, Malcolm X, was running out of time.

*   *   *

The summer of 1963 was a season of revolution. Boycotts and protests in the South were becoming increasingly violent. In Mississippi, threats against protesters and civil rights activists turned deadly. On June 12, 1963, Medgar Evers, a field secretary for the NAACP, was killed by a white supremacist. Segregationists had been attacking activists and protesters for years. They believed that Black people did not deserve any civil rights. They were especially angry that Black citizens wanted to vote, a right they thought would give them too much power.

The revolution was concentrated not only in the American South. In the North, Black people protested unfair living conditions. Many had left the South for better jobs and opportunities but found that all forms of racism and poor housing options existed in the North as well. Malcolm X used his platform to draw attention to the persistent racial inequalities north of the Mason-Dixon Line. He also criticized southern Christian civil rights leaders, such as Martin Luther King Jr., for compromising with a United States government that never lived up to its promises of protecting Black rights.

On August 10, 1963, in the streets of Harlem, Malcolm X spoke to a large audience about the upcoming

March on Washington for Jobs and Freedom. The Nation of Islam, he said, would not participate in the racially integrated march. An undercover agent from the NYPD's Bureau of Special Services spied Cassius Clay at the rally, listening closely to Malcolm X. As Cassius and Malcolm grew closer, it became more dangerous for the boxer to be seen with the minister.

The March on Washington was, nevertheless, an unprecedented demonstration for racial equality. On August 28, 1963, more than two thousand buses, twenty-one special trains, ten chartered flights, and armies of cars converged on Washington, DC, for the historic occasion—one of the largest civil rights protests in US history.

The march placed Martin Luther King at the head of the Civil Rights Movement, and his iconic speech "I Have A Dream" quickly became an international cry for freedom and equality. Malcolm X held firm on his position against the march. He pointed out that just one month after the historic event, the Ku Klux Klan bombed a church in Birmingham, killing four little girls. As a father of three girls, with one on the way, Malcolm imagined that it was his daughters taken in the senseless murder. Malcolm was furious, pointing out that

Martin's nonviolent protest had once again put innocent Black children in harm's way. The bombing was a brutal reminder, he said, that the march had failed.

He told a reporter, "Now that the show is over, the black masses are still without land, without jobs, and without homes.... Their Christian churches are still being bombed, their innocent little girls murdered." So, Malcolm said to the writer, "What did the March on Washington accomplish? Nothing!"

Since July 1963, when a reporter from the *Chicago Sun-Times* caught Cassius Clay leaving one of the Nation of Islam's schools, writers had been investigating his involvement with the Black Muslims, searching for clues about his relationship with Malcolm X. Although Cassius denied any involvement with the Nation, when he was asked about civil rights, he had said it was the "law of nature" that people "should associate with their own kind."

Listening to Cassius, reporters detected the Nation's influence on his evolving identity. In the past, he had proclaimed that he would save boxing because he was the most talented and entertaining fighter in the world. Yet as he listened to Elijah Muhammad and spent more time with Malcolm X, Cassius began thinking of himself as divine, graced by the power of Allah. "I am the resurrection, I am the prophet," he declared. Hearing Elijah and Malcolm preach about Black superiority and the power of true believers affirmed what Cassius had always thought about himself: that he *was* the greatest.

In September, Cassius traveled to Philadelphia to attend Elijah's first public lecture of the year. More than six thousand people packed the arena. Cassius listened intently as the Messenger denounced white men for harming Black people. Elijah insisted that the very survival of Black people required that they separate from white people. Throughout his lecture, Cassius rose to his feet, loudly applauding. Near the end of the rally, an NOI official asked the boxer to stand in front of the audience and be recognized. At that moment, even before he had won the heavyweight championship, Cassius became a publicity tool for the Nation. He was a visible symbol of the movement at a time when Black folks were increasingly fed up with the Nation of Islam's failure to improve the conditions of Black citizens.

No one heard this criticism more than Malcolm. But he knew Elijah would never change tactics. What the Nation needed, then, was an infusion of energy and youth, a figure who personified Black strength, a voice that could be heard above all the noise. So when Cassius Clay received a standing ovation in Philadelphia, a stirring sound that Malcolm had heard only at Madison Square Garden, he knew that he had found the Nation's new symbol, a force that could grow the movement.

Yet the boxer was not prepared for such a publicity role. After the rally ended, reporters rushed toward Cassius, but he was in no mood to answer their questions. "If you want to interview somebody, interview Malcolm X," he said. "He's really got something important to say." The newsmen were stunned that for the first time in memory Cassius did not want to talk. He departed the arena without saying much, worried that the media's investigations into his relationship with the Nation might harm his shot at the title.

Cassius did not realize that Malcolm had bigger plans for him. Nor could he have foreseen that the rally in Philadelphia would be the last time he would ever see Malcolm and Elijah together onstage. From his third-row seat, he witnessed Muhammad bestow a great honor upon Malcolm, naming him national minister. But this appointment was just another test, a challenge for Malcolm to prove that he really was Elijah's "most faithful, hard-working minister." What Cassius saw that day—a kingdom in harmony—was a mirage. He heard Muhammad close his remarks with an eerily prophetic promise: Malcolm, Elijah said, "will follow me until he dies."

By November, Malcolm X desperately wanted to join in the action of organizing and protesting injustice, but Elijah Muhammad would not allow it. Malcolm struggled to keep quiet. He spent time thinking about his future and what he'd do about Elijah Muhammad. Months after he'd confronted the Messenger about his secret families and lies, the minister still had not accepted that his leader was a fraud. Elijah had asked him not to mention his secret families to the other Muslim ministers—he did not want more members to know about his infidelities.

Even though Malcolm agreed to keep quiet at the time, he did tell other ministers about Elijah's faults. He wanted them to know what was going on so that they could prepare for when, or if, the secrets ever went public. Malcolm X confided in his friend Louis X, later known as Louis Farrakhan, a minister in Boston. He felt that Louis and a few other ministers would keep the information safe. Malcolm was still unsure of his place in the organization and how he would move forward.

He'd made a home in the Nation of Islam and had found a father figure in Elijah Muhammad. However, he knew that he could not support a man who led a double life— preaching one thing and doing another. Malcolm would have to make a firm decision if he was going to stay with the Nation of Islam or a decision would be made for him.

If the minister's loyalty to Elijah Muhammad was in doubt, Cassius Clay's to Malcom was not. Cassius found his sanctuary visiting Malcolm X in Harlem at Temple No. 7. Since Cassius returned from London that summer, his relationship with Malcolm had deepened. He solicited his mentor's advice about all things, spiritual and professional. "Malcolm," he said later, "was very intelligent, with a good sense of humor, a wise man. When he talked, he held me spellbound for hours."

In their private moments together, the two men forged a friendship, a bond, a brotherhood. Cassius adored Malcolm and treated him like an older brother. He swelled with pride whenever the minister was near. Malcolm treated him like a man whose thoughts mattered, not like an athlete whose only merit was his body. Cassius, he observed, was "sensitive, very humble, yet shrewd."

Malcolm was not the only person keeping a sharp eye on Cassius. A New York news columnist reported that

Cassius wore the NOI membership ring and flaunted a picture of himself and Elijah Muhammad. The Louisville Sponsoring Group (LSG), Cassius's managers, were concerned by these reports. They'd hoped to draw Cassius away from Malcolm by sending him overseas to fight, but instead Cassius was distancing himself from the LSG members and his wealthy white benefactors. He was also reluctant to return to Florida to train with Dundee. The LSG frantically enlisted promoters, sponsors, and even Cassius's mother to persuade him to return to his boxing life in Miami.

Reporters and members of the Louisville Sponsoring Group were not the only ones interested in Cassius's involvement with the Nation. The FBI's Chicago office had Elijah Muhammad's mansion under surveillance, and Bureau officials believed their spying had "proven extremely valuable in covering the overall activities of the NOI." The Bureau's agents had learned about the sect's vulnerabilities and discovered that Cassius Clay, "the well-known heavyweight title contender, had made arrangements to meet Elijah Muhammad and to also have his parents meet The Messenger." Clearly Malcolm X was not the only powerful figure courting Clay— Elijah Muhammad also grasped the boxer's propaganda value for the Nation's cause. If Cassius Clay finally dethroned Sonny Liston as the heavyweight champion, it would prove the righteousness of the Nation of Islam and confirm Muhammad's power to bless those who followed him.

On November 22, 1963, the country was shocked to a halt as news spread that President John F. Kennedy had been assassinated in Dallas. President Kennedy was young and popular, and the entire country mourned his death. Elijah Muhammad released a statement expressing his disappointment over the tragedy. He also told his followers not to comment on it. He didn't want any negative publicity and feared someone may blame the Nation of Islam for the president's death. America was grieving; it was no time for politics or finger pointing. Once again, Malcolm X couldn't help but express his opinions. When reporters asked for his thoughts, Malcolm's commentary was cruel: The president's murder was a case of "chickens coming home to roost... Chickens coming home to roost never did make me sad; they've always made me glad."

It was no secret that Malcolm did not support President Kennedy. He blamed him for enabling anti-Black violence in the South and thought the president and the CIA were responsible for assassinating Vietnamese and Congolese politicians. However, disparaging a beloved president so soon after his tragic death was too much for the American public to handle—and too much for Elijah Muhammad. All of Malcolm's critics in the Nation called Elijah and said that this time Malcolm had gone too far, and the aging leader agreed. Of all the mistakes Malcolm may have made in his career, this was by far the worst. His shocking comments not only put the Nation under close watch by the FBI but also proved what Elijah's children and close advisers had been saying all along: Malcolm was unpredictable and could not be trusted.

Elijah summoned Malcolm to Chicago to discuss his mistake. Malcolm knew that he would be punished, but he had no idea how severely. He expected Elijah to be furious, but what he encountered instead was a calm man disappointed in one of his favorite followers. After scolding Malcolm, Elijah decided to silence Malcolm for ninety days. The minister was forbidden from speaking to the press and from preaching at meetings.

Malcolm could not object to his punishment. He knew his actions were terribly wrong, but being silenced that way felt impossible to accept. Malcolm's identity was built around his ability to speak with power and influence. Being quiet meant that he could not be himself. The media quickly picked up on tensions within the Nation. Journalists falsely reported that the Nation would split into two factions: one in Chicago following Elijah Muhammad, and another based in New York City, led by Malcolm X. Malcolm tried to ignore the gossip. He focused on ways to get back on Elijah's good side. If he could only show how sorry he was, his punishment might not last a whole three months. Malcolm was hopeful and committed to the faith, but in Chicago, Muhammad's suspicions against Malcolm grew.

Elijah learned that some of the East Coast ministers knew about his secret families from Malcolm. The Messenger was not living the honest life he preached about. Elijah was furious—he had asked Malcolm to protect his secrets. In fact, he had asked for Malcolm's discretion as a test to see if he could really trust him. Malcolm failed the test—and Muhammad knew he was unmanageable. If he couldn't steer his most popular minister, he would surely lose control of his organization. Elijah sent word to his trusted leaders to cut ties with Malcolm X. Anyone who took Malcolm's side became Muhammad's—and the Nation's—enemy. Some of Elijah's most loyal followers escalated the hostility to threats against Malcolm's life and even the lives of his family. Muhammad, who once treated Malcolm like a son, was now intent on destroying him—all because Malcolm had dared to tell the truth about Elijah's harmful lies.

Malcolm was shattered. He had looked up to Elijah Muhammad and credited him with rescuing him from a life that lacked purpose. Now they were nothing but strangers. Malcolm tried to reason with the Messenger, but Elijah was intent on stripping him down and making him suffer. Instead of a ninety-day punishment, Muhammad banished him from the Nation indefinitely.

This suspension meant that Malcolm could no longer earn money to take care of his wife and daughters. He had no savings, insurance, or property. The house he and his family lived in was owned by the Nation of Islam. This punishment was the final blow to an already strained relationship. Malcolm knew that his time in the Nation was coming to an end but he wasn't sure what his Muslim brothers would do. Living in complete isolation from his community, Malcolm began to worry. He knew what happened to disobedient followers. At this point, Malcolm X was surrounded by men who strictly obeyed Elijah Muhammad's orders, even if those orders were to hurt him.

Malcolm began to think of ways to get out of this mess. Could he benefit from his relationship with Cassius Clay? Malcolm knew that Cassius was very important to the Nation's cause. Cassius was young, rich, and famous. His popularity made him a magnet for new members. Cassius and Malcolm were friends, but would he leave the Nation and follow Malcolm, considering this rift?

Malcolm decided that the only way for him to survive was to attach himself to Cassius; and he'd have to act quickly. Wherever Cassius went, Malcolm needed to be right there next to him. He wanted Elijah Muhammad to see him with Cassius, to prove to the Messenger that at least one famous person had not forgotten the minister. Their public bond would also challenge Elijah Muhammad's order that members of the Nation could not interact with Malcolm. Muhammad would be forced either to accept Malcolm back into the fold or to punish Cassius. But the boxer was a star in the organization, so maybe the Messenger would opt to let the disgraced minister back into the movement. It was a dangerous plan hinged on defiance—but there was nothing left for Malcolm X to lose.

CHAPTER SEVEN

TROUBLE IN MIAMI

They had better stop him or I will.
Enough is enough.

—*Sonny Liston*

By the end of 1963, trouble seemed to follow Malcolm X wherever he went. In New York, his mind was filled with thoughts of Elijah Muhammad. His phone rang constantly with reporters asking about his future in the Nation. Malcolm was unsure what to tell them. The FBI also contacted him. They wanted to know if he was done with Elijah Muhammad for good, and if the Nation had plans to harm the new president, Lyndon Johnson. The incessant calls and harassment were weighing him down.

Malcolm couldn't visit his usual spots in Harlem because many of his friends had turned their backs on him following Elijah's orders. Malcolm was heartbroken.

He poured his thoughts and feelings into autobiography writing sessions with Alex Haley. The writer wanted Malcolm to talk more about his childhood and how he became such a fierce leader. But Malcolm couldn't take his mind off the future. Alex and Malcolm spent many nights talking about his life and what would happen if Malcolm was never able to rejoin the Nation. Haley didn't know it then, but the book he and Malcolm were working on would give the world a glimpse into the minister's deepest hopes and fears.

In January 1964, Malcolm decided to take a family trip to Miami, where Cassius was training for his upcoming duel against Sonny Liston. Malcolm needed time away from New York and hoped to focus more on his relationship with Cassius. As soon as he made arrangements, the FBI notified their Miami agents. The government had been tapping Malcolm's calls and following him for months, ever suspicious of the minister's power and politics. Cassius was happy for his friend to come visit. He also loved Malcolm's wife, Betty, and their little girls. Once Malcolm and his family arrived at Miami's

Hampton House motel, Cassius's old friend Sam Saxon spotted them. He was surprised to see Malcolm, especially since the title fight was more than a month away. He also knew that Malcolm was suspended from the Nation. Malcolm wasn't supposed to be close with other Black Muslims. Saxon quickly grew suspicious.

Cassius spent a lot of time with Malcolm that month. When he wasn't training, he'd visit the Hampton House and play with Malcolm's three daughters. "I liked him," Malcolm admitted. "Betty liked him. Our children were crazy about him." Watching her husband interact with Cassius, Betty could see that Malcolm "loved him like a younger brother."

It seemed that Miami was the one place where Malcolm could finally relax and escape his troubles. He began to think that he and Cassius could make a good team. In the early evenings, they walked the streets of Miami while undercover FBI agents trailed closely behind them. In those conversations, Malcolm learned that Cassius was an inquisitive young man who absorbed everything he taught him. Malcolm also recognized that Cassius's unique ability to generate publicity could transform the boxer into a political force—someone who could unify a human rights movement at home and abroad. Whether

Malcolm returned to the Nation or not, Cassius was ideally suited to follow him and to use his platform as a boxer to organize Black Americans in the fight for justice and equality.

Back at the NOI headquarters in Chicago, NOI officials were growing irritated that Malcolm and Cassius were together in Miami. Although Malcolm wanted Elijah Muhammad to see him with Cassius so that he could demonstrate his importance in the boxer's life, deep down, he must have known that he would never reconcile with the Messenger or return to the Nation. He wrote Elijah letters pleading for reinstatement but never received a written reply. Elijah's silence told Malcolm all he needed to know.

Contemplating his uncertain future, Malcolm spent days talking with Cassius about destiny. While most folks doubted that Cassius would defeat Sonny Liston, Malcolm was a believer. He encouraged Cassius and boosted his inner strength. Malcolm told Cassius that he was too smart, too fast, and too strong to lose this fight. It was everything Cassius needed to hear. Malcolm explained that this heavyweight championship was not just a regular fight, but that Cassius was part of Allah's plan. The minister thought that the boxer just might be like the holy men he'd learned about during his childhood, the ones God spoke to. Cassius received Malcolm's words as though they were a message from God.

All this talk of Allah made Dundee concerned. The only thing Dundee knew about Malcolm X was what he read in the papers: He didn't like white people and spoke ill of the late President Kennedy. Meanwhile, Malcolm made himself at home at the 5th Street Gym, watching Cassius train. When reporters came to see Cassius, he would make sure to talk to them. When photographers took pictures of Cassius, Malcolm wiggled his way in front of the camera, too. He always had a smile on his face, which Dundee found more threatening than a frown. Malcolm's presence made him nervous. He thought the minister was up to something but didn't know what it was.

Dundee began to lose patience with Cassius. They were a month away from the biggest fight of his career, and instead of focusing on the sport, he was spending too much time with Malcolm. He expressed his concerns to the fighter, but Cassius ignored him. It seemed that Cassius trusted guidance from only the Black Muslims. He even asked Malcolm X for training advice in the ring!

Dundee wasn't the only one upset with Cassius. Odessa Clay, the boxer's mother, thought that the Black

Muslims had brainwashed her sons. She said that the Nation of Islam turned her children against women, white people, and even their mother. Cassius Clay Sr. also didn't trust the Nation of Islam in the least. He was upset upon learning that his son Rudy had traded their family name for X. In the Nation's traditional style of new membership, Rudy was now Rudy X. Little did they know that, by this time, Cassius had also traded in Clay for X.

The Clay family grew up with Christian principles and felt threatened as outsiders to the Nation of Islam. Cassius tried to appease his parents' concerns and dispel the rumors that Black Muslims did not like white people. The boxer even told reporters that the Nation of Islam rejected hatred, instead teaching Black history and giving him pride in his identity. Regardless, Clay's parents weren't the only people in his life skeptical of the Nation.

The Louisville Sponsoring Group didn't want Clay's new affiliates to compromise any earnings. They still made money off Clay from his boxing matches. Attempting to redeem Cassius's public image, the sponsors set up a sparring match to raise money for a charity benefiting cerebral palsy. This was the perfect opportunity to remind the public he was "just a nice, sweet kid." Cassius smiled and sparred for the cameras at this event, but his sponsors still worried about how to separate the boxer from Malcolm X and the Nation of Islam more permanently. Cassius had no intention to leave the organization. Meanwhile, between Malcolm X and Elijah Muhammad, the Nation had big plans for their prizefighter.

By February 1964, with a few weeks left until the heavyweight title match, Cassius Clay began to refocus on Sonny Liston. He needed to knock Sonny off his game. Cassius had verbally attacked Sonny several times, traveling to his home and harassing him outside the gym. It was all part of Cassius's psychological strategy, and Sonny quickly clued in to the performance. Just as quickly, Sonny grew tired of it all—he couldn't escape Cassius in any part of his life. In North Miami, Sonny had a cinematic training program with lights, music, and a beautiful ocean view. He charged an entry fee of fifty cents for anyone interested in watching him train. The production began with about twenty minutes of film showcasing Sonny's winning fight against Floyd. Once the video ended, Sonny was revealed, standing still and expressionless. He was a massive man, and his stern face rising above the crowd on the elevated stage made him look terrifying. Sonny would then begin his workout,

shadowboxing and gliding across the ring with a sparring partner. He'd even play music while jumping rope
or throwing weighted balls with his trainer. It was a great
performance, and a chance for the champ to display his
athletic ability. However, Cassius would soon turn Sonny's show into a mockery.

Cassius had threatened to crash the routine plenty
of times. But on February 7, he showed up wearing a
"Bear Huntin'" jacket and carrying a walking stick. He
and his friends crashed the show. Cassius had always
called Sonny a big bear, referring to his imposing size.
The champion usually let insults roll off his back, but
that day he just wasn't in the mood. Liston said somebody better stop Clay or he would do it himself. The
constant insults and public criticisms were starting to
wear down the hardened fighter. He could endure the
public's disdain, but it was hard not to react to the constant disrespect from Cassius Clay. This form of taunting
was unprecedented. In the past, boxers kept the fighting
in the ring. As violent as the sport could be, there was
still a code of respect. Sonny had worked hard to earn
that respect. He grew up in poverty, spent two years in
prison, and had become the heavyweight champion of
the world. Sonny was unable to read or write but was

proud of his accomplishments. Whether people liked him or not, Sonny Liston deserved respect. And Cassius Clay was the most disrespectful peer he had ever met.

Unaffected by his sponsors' concerns, Cassius continued to act independently. He kept pestering Sonny and causing chaos between them. He also continued to appear publicly, in photos, with the Nation of Islam—most notably with Malcolm X—which made the boxer much less popular. Notably, Miami's Jewish community threatened to boycott the fight because of Cassius's involvement with the disgraced Muslim minister. Malcolm X had previously accused Jews of exploiting Black athletes for profit, a suggestion that offended many people.

Finally, the boxing officials had enough. They called Cassius in for a meeting and gave him an ultimatum: Denounce the Black Muslims or cancel the championship fight against Sonny Liston. This was a brutal decision. Cassius had found a family in the Nation of Islam that he couldn't give up: "My religion is more important to me than the fight," he said. With that proclamation, the much-anticipated match was canceled.

This news was shocking to all. Cassius had worked so hard to get to the top of the sport. He'd even predicted his win. Yet he was willing to sacrifice that dream for Elijah Muhammad. The boxing officials called the sales and publicity team to tell them the news. Fortunately, they said that it was too late to cancel the fight. They had already sold thousands of tickets and signed contracts to broadcast the event in theaters across America. Organizers faced a dilemma: They couldn't imagine hosting the fight while Cassius was losing public support for opposing integration—a core principle of the NOI. But, practically, they couldn't cancel because they'd lose too much money by having to return any presold tickets.

Considering this challenge, publicist Harold Conrad had a great idea. He knew the biggest problem for Cassius's image was Malcolm X. If Malcolm left Miami for a while, perhaps the fight could go on—and no one would lose any money. Harold decided to speak with the minister. He drove to Cassius's home, where he was met by a group of quiet Muslim men. Cassius was in no mood to talk, but Harold was focused on Malcolm. He explained that the fight was at stake and told Malcolm that he had the power to save Cassius's career simply by leaving town. Malcolm stood silently, considering Harold's plea.

Finally, Malcolm X agreed to leave Miami but promised he would be back to attend the fight. It was the right thing to do and Malcolm didn't want to hurt Cassius in any way. The fighter soon learned that Malcolm had saved the day—the fight was back on. However, Cassius had something else on his mind, something he was keeping from Malcolm. Cassius had recently spoken to Elijah Muhammad, who reminded his follower that Malcolm was still punished and should be shunned. Any Muslim who disobeyed Muhammad would be punished, too. Cassius did not want to disappoint the Messenger, but Malcolm was his close friend. He recognized this conversation as a gentle warning from Elijah, and Cassius knew perfectly well how angry he could get when someone disobeyed him. Soon, Cassius would be forced to choose between his friend Malcolm X and his leader, Elijah Muhammad.

Two days before the fight, Sonny had finished training and was at home resting before the big day. His Florida beach house was on Biscayne Bay, an area surrounded by water. Sonny enjoyed his peace, while he still could. He liked to relax with his thoughts before a big fight. Reporters were curious about his state of mind. They called him for a quote, but the champ didn't have much to say. Sonny didn't much care for the media, unlike his gregarious opponent, Cassius. Former champion Joe Louis, a close friend, had his own predictions about the fight. Like many critics, Joe thought that Cassius was a good fighter but no match for Sonny. In 1964, Sonny seemed invincible. In his three previous fights, he had knocked out his opponents in the first round. Critics thought Cassius would go down the same way.

A short drive away from Biscayne Bay, Cassius was also preparing for the fight. Instead of the quiet, peaceful atmosphere of Sonny's beach property, Cassius's home— a small house in a busy Black neighborhood—was filled with people in constant motion. He made neighbors, friends, and visitors feel welcome whenever they came by. An assistant to Cassius Clay would regularly set up a makeshift movie theater outside his home, where Cassius entertained the kids in the area by doing playful voice-overs for movies. Neighbors loved him for it— they'd watch horror films as Cassius acted out the plot, sprinkling in laughs along the way. A few sportswriters visited Cassius's home and described it as chaos. They were uncomfortable about the men in dark suits and bow ties who stared at them intensely, quickly realizing these people were from the brotherhood, the Nation of Islam. They viewed the reporters not as guests but as trespassers on private property.

The day before the historic fight, Malcolm returned to Miami as promised and Cassius picked him up at the airport. As soon as Malcolm got in the car, Cassius asked, "Any word from Chicago?" He wanted to know if Elijah had forgiven Malcolm yet. Without hesitation, Malcolm simply replied, "Nothing positive." Malcolm's response didn't convey the whole truth. He had heard from Elijah, who was based in Chicago, the Nation of Islam's headquarters. Muhammad's secretary had informed Malcolm that he was still suspended. Outwardly, the minister was cool as ever. If he was nervous about being ostracized, he sure didn't let anyone—especially Cassius—know. He believed that his future depended on Cassius Clay's success, and he could not risk upsetting the boxer so close to the fight.

Malcolm thought that surely Allah had brought Cassius into his life for a reason. He just had to convince Elijah Muhammad that Cassius was sent to them for a purpose, too. He contacted the Nation's headquarters again to convey his grand vision: Cassius would win the heavyweight championship, and his new reigning title would make him the Nation's most important new member. Cassius was valuable and could bring in a lot of new members. The minister and the fighter were a package deal, a friendship that would command attention across the world. Malcolm X could deliver this powerful combination to Muhammad, if only he'd let him back into the Nation of Islam.

Once again, Malcolm was rejected. The Nation's leaders didn't believe Cassius would win. Sure, he was popular and a good boxer, but he was up against a true legend and had no chance. Malcolm did not anticipate that Elijah had his own secret plans for Cassius Clay: If Cassius lost, he'd remain a competitive, if not champion, boxer, but he could still be useful. In the unlikely scenario that Cassius happened to win, the NOI leaders would push Malcolm X to the side and reap all the benefits of having a huge celebrity to themselves.

Hours away from the fight, Cassius was back to his old provocation tricks. This time he had his friends play along. Wearing his trusty "Bear Huntin'" jacket, he burst into a meeting room. Assistant trainer Bundini Brown was with him. Together they began to yell, "Float like a butterfly and sting like a bee—rumble, young man, rumble!" They repeated the lines over and over, turning the words into an iconic chant that would define boxing history. Bundini was like a battery charger for Cassius. He amped him up and gave him energy. Cassius didn't stop at the chanting. He boasted about beating Sonny in eight rounds, and even insulted Joe Louis.

Cassius and Bundini went on and on until one of Cassius's sponsors interrupted the chaos with a sobering reminder: If Cassius didn't stop, he'd be fined. The challenger and his trainer went back to their dressing room, awaiting his time to weigh in. Nevertheless, anyone who thought the threat of a fine would stop Cassius Clay would be terribly mistaken. Hundreds of reporters had lined up to witness the preliminary weigh-in, where athletes registered their final weight before the match. This event also marked the last time the boxers would meet before showtime. Tension between the opponents was a guarantee. As Cassius moved toward the platform for the officials to take his weight, Sonny emerged from his dressing room. Cassius exploded: "Hey, sucker, you a chump," he said. "Are you scared?" He hollered and promised that someone was going to die in the ring. Cassius was out of control. Even Bundini tried to get him to calm down. Cassius continued, threatening Sonny in a room full of reporters and officials for the event.

Liston didn't pay much attention to all the commotion. He was used to Cassius's hostility. He decided to toss a few words back, which riled up Cassius even more. Cassius acted like he was going to hit Sonny, and four or five men tried to hold him back. Amid this struggle, Cassius winked at his boxer friend, Sugar Ray Robinson. The wink signaled to Sugar Ray that Cassius was under control—this scuffle was all just for show. Finally, Cassius got down to business for the weigh-in.

Sonny weighed 218 pounds, while Cassius was a bit over 210. Next, officials monitored the boxers' pulses, which would tell them how fast each person's heart was beating and ensure the men were healthy enough to compete. Sonny's heart rate registered at 80 beats per minute. It was just a little higher than his usual rate of 72. Cassius, however, was at 120—through the roof! This number alarmed doctors and officials in the room, who inferred that his heart was racing because he was afraid. Cassius must have worried that Sonny would hurt him.

Rumors began to circulate that Cassius was scared of Liston. This became yet another reason for fans and critics to believe that he had no chance of winning. Nearly sixty writers picked Sonny to win the fight by a knockout before the end of the third round. They predicted the match would be a slaughter, with Sonny the butcher winning easily. The only people who went on record picking Cassius were his family and Malcolm X. The minister spoke respectfully, even lovingly, about Cassius, highlighting his intellectual and emotional attributes. The boxer was kind, gentle, humble, nothing like the man who clowned for the press. But Malcolm thought Cassius's greatest gift was his political instinct: "He should be a diplomat. He has the instinct of seeing a tricky situation shaping up...and resolving how to side-step it."

Very few people shared Malcolm's faith that Cassius Clay would become the next champion. Not even Elijah Muhammad went on record to support Cassius. But Cassius looked at the match as a chance to prove the doubters wrong. No matter what his critics—or his heart rate—said, Cassius knew he would win the fight. Malcolm X explained to a reporter, "To be a Muslim is to know no fear." Cassius had something that Sonny didn't have: Allah.

CHAPTER EIGHT

FIGHT NIGHT

> Nobody walks away from a heavyweight championship.
>
> *—Angelo Dundee*

Finally, the moment had arrived. Cassius Clay was ready to shake up the world and upset Sonny Liston in a heavyweight championship fight. After praying with Cassius in the dressing room, Malcolm X geared up for the match in his lucky seat: row seven, seat seven. According to the Nation of Islam's numerology, three numbers were special for Black people: seven, twelve, and twenty-one. Malcolm knew this alignment was just another confirmation from Allah that Cassius Clay would be the heavyweight champion of the world.

Cassius entered the ring wearing a short white robe. He had seen some of his celebrity friends in the Golden Circle seats, the high-priced section close to the ring. Cassius had a plan. He knew that Sonny had won his last three fights by a quick knockout. Cassius planned to tire out his opponent early on. He would make him chase him, always dodging Sonny's hard left hand. Cassius knew that Sonny was overconfident and hadn't trained very hard. He was used to knocking opponents out in the first round, and most critics thought this, too, would be an easy win for him. If Cassius could get Sonny past the third round, the champion would be exhausted and wear himself out. Once Sonny was tired, he'd lose his focus and start throwing wild punches. Cassius thought the strategy would help him get to the eighth round, where he could shake Sonny up and catch him off guard. It was a smart plan, but Sonny wouldn't be as predictable as Cassius had hoped.

As he waited for the opening bell, Cassius danced from left to right foot. On the other side of the ring, Sonny scraped his feet against the canvas, menacingly preparing to charge. The bell rang, and both fighters headed for the center of the ring. Cassius moved around, circling instead of taking a straight path toward his target. Sonny had a hard time landing a punch. For the first half of the round, Cassius hardly threw a punch. It was all part of his plan to run down the champ. Cassius moved gracefully around the ring, while Sonny looked unsure of himself. Finally, Cassius saw an opportunity. He began to punch and jab, stopping Sonny from getting closer to him. Sonny became angry that he wasn't landing any punches. He charged at Cassius, throwing punches even after the bell rang at the end of round one.

The crowd was surprised to see Cassius doing so well. Every time Sonny missed a punch, spectators would let out a sound of disappointment. In the second round, Sonny grew more aggressive. He threw more body punches, hoping to slow Cassius down. However, he didn't have much luck reaching his opponent's body. Cassius stayed a safe distance away from the champ, focusing instead on Sonny's eyes. Sometimes you can tell what a person is about to do by watching the eyes or facial expressions. Cassius quickly learned that Sonny "eyed him up" whenever he was on the verge of throwing a heavy punch. Cassius recognized the pattern and was better prepared to move, anticipating a punch. As

Cassius ducked and slid, he soon saw an opening. Sonny had a bruise on his cheek. A few sharp punches would split the bruise open and cause him to bleed. This was a big discovery. Critics, fans, and even Sonny himself didn't think the champion could bleed. He'd always been a powerhouse on offense, and people generally feared him. Cassius wanted to prove that the boxing giant was still vulnerable. And if he could be hurt, it was just a matter of time before he could be defeated.

As the third round began, Cassius threw and landed the first punches. He saw that Sonny was hurt and confused. Cassius had not planned to jump into action so soon, but he didn't want to waste any time. Suddenly, Sonny's cheek split open. It began to bleed. Cassius had done it! He didn't hesitate to keep throwing punches— left hook, right hook—all while the crowd roared in excitement. Everyone was on their feet as the announcers narrated a blow-by-blow: "Sonny wobbled! Cassius has him hurt!...Sonny's cut below the eye! And he's getting hit with all the punches in the book!" Sonny was furious. As soon as he saw the blood on his gloves, he rushed toward Cassius. Throwing all his weight into wild punches, the champ crashed painfully into Cassius's body. Because he was reacting out of anger, many of his punches missed—again. Sonny looked clumsy, as if he were struggling to find his way through a dark room.

The crowd stood at attention, amazed at what they were witnessing. Sonny was no match for Cassius's quick hands and feet. He was tired and often leaned on the ropes for support. According to some critics, the once-overconfident champ looked frightened. Maybe Sonny thought this fight was the end of his reign, but he didn't give up. Cassius stood far away from him, yelling, "Come on! Come on, you bum!" As Cassius kept moving around the ring, looking energetic and confident, some ringside fans thought that Sonny was finished. Cassius was showing them exactly what he'd promised: that he was worthy of the championship title. But Cassius had not yet displayed the full range of his skill. The next round would prove once and for all that the young boxer was ready for anything.

As the third-round closing bell rang, Sonny went to his corner. It was clear that he was exhausted and injured. His trainers cleaned him up and nurtured his wound. Then something happened. Sonny's team put a blinding substance on his gloves. This would compromise any opponent, making it hard to see if the substance got near the eyes. Sportswriter Jack McKinney, sitting near Sonny's corner, overheard the heavyweight champion directing his team to "juice the gloves," authorizing this illegal trick. This wouldn't be the first time Sonny was accused of fighting dirty. Previous Liston opponents had also complained that something painful had gotten in their eyes during their fights.

Cassius dominated the fourth round. However, by the time the bell rang, he was in pain: His face hurt and his eyes burned as if there were acid in them. He could barely see. Cassius immediately thought that someone was trying to fix the fight against him. He screamed that something was wrong, Liston was fighting dirty! Dundee did not want to forfeit the fight. He knew that Cassius was primed for the heavyweight title, he just needed to finish. He quickly examined him and wiped his eyes. When Cassius still complained of pain, Dundee put his pinky in his eye and then put it in his own as a test. His eye immediately began to burn. The coach also sniffed and tasted the towel that he'd used to wipe Cassius's eyes, and it tasted strange. Now Dundee was certain that Sonny's team had cheated, but he couldn't stop the fight. Instead, he pivoted to a solution, sponging the boxer's eyes and trying to flush out the toxins. He told Cassius, "Nobody walks away form a heavyweight championship."

The pain would pass and he'd have to fight through it, keeping away from Sonny until his eyes cleared.

While Dundee focused on getting Cassius back in the game, the Muslims at ringside were drawing their own conclusion. They heard Cassius mention that something was wrong and got out of their seats to watch Dundee wipe the boxer's eyes. Dundee seemed to be responsible for Cassius's pain, and the Black Muslim spectators were furious. To quickly prove his innocence, Dundee wiped his face with the same towel he used on Cassius. He was trying to keep the peace, but his first priority was always Cassius. When the bell rang for round five, Dundee pushed the boxer forward and shouted that this was his moment: "We aren't going to quit now!...Run until your eyes clear! Run!"

Cassius kept moving, nearly blinded and visibly confused. His friend Bundini was also in the corner, encouraging him: "Yardstick 'im, champ! Yardstick 'im!" It was great advice. He wanted Cassius to keep his distance from Sonny until he regained his vision. In past fights, Cassius had used his left hand, held straight out, as a yardstick for measuring distance and punches. If ever there was a time to use the yardstick strategy, this was it.

Sonny saw that Cassius was struggling, making this

the optimal time to strike. He rushed forward like a menacing school bully. Cassius moved backward but was unable to avoid Sonny's powerful attack. Instead, he grabbed his opponent and held on. This stopped Sonny from throwing his hardest punches while allowing Cassius to give Sonny a few jabs to the body. Sonny fought back hard, using every ounce of his strength to attack Cassius's body up close. He punished Cassius for embarrassing him during the first round and for all the taunts and name-calling. Cassius absorbed Sonny's body shots. He needed clear eyes to avoid punches and to see when Sonny would strike. Now his best assets were compromised. Cassius's ability to take a punch was the only thing keeping him in the ring.

Using up all his strength, Sonny got tired again during the fifth round. He started throwing fewer, slower punches and rested more often by leaning on Cassius and hugging him. The challenger had endured a beating but realized it was coming to an end. He got away from Sonny and began to yardstick him. He yelled, "You ain't nothing!" and slapped him lightly a few times. Cassius showed that, even through intense pain, he still had the energy to taunt his opponents. The bell soon rang, allowing both fighters to take a much-needed rest. For Sonny, the end of the round marked his last chance to beat Cassius. He had given all he had, he had fought dirty, and still he was outmatched. The champ had nothing left.

As he prepared for round six, Cassius felt a second wind. His eyes cleared and he saw that his opponent was exhausted. He knew that Sonny just couldn't take much more. Cassius's confidence grew, encouraged by Dundee, who told him to get mad, to go knock Sonny out for all that he had done. As the bell rang for round six, he'd already planned to make Sonny pay. He got closer to Sonny and began to box slower. He wanted every move to count. Cassius used his skills to land jabs, punch combinations, or hooks. He would back away before Sonny had a chance to respond. Cassius looked great in the ring, and he wanted to make sure the media noticed, too. Between punches, he turned around to face the press and told them, "I'm gonna upset the world!" The reporters couldn't believe what they were witnessing. Cassius was taunting them while fighting the heavyweight champion—and he was making it look easy. And while the reporters and many in the crowd were shocked to see the fight unfolding in favor of Cassius Clay, Malcolm X had always believed.

Sonny lost his confidence. By the end of the sixth

round, he decided he would not leave his corner. His team signaled to officials that the fight was over—Sonny Liston was through. Later on, they would insist that Sonny had torn a tendon in his left arm early in the fight, making it too painful to compete. Sonny's team also said that ending the match was a management decision, that Sonny had wanted to continue the fight and defend his title. Regardless, Sonny's team still ended the fight, which meant that a new heavyweight champion would be crowned.

Cassius knew what was happening before the referee officially called it. He was looking right at Sonny when the last warning buzzer sounded. Cassius raised both arms high in the air and broke into a dance. He floated to the center of the ring, where Bundini hugged him. This didn't last long because, of course, Cassius had a message for the press, "I am the greatest! I shook up the world!" He told reporters that they should be ashamed of betting against him. Cassius had predicted he would win, believed it, and thought that Allah had ordained it. This time, no one could deny the new heavyweight world champion his right to brag.

At just twenty-two years old, Cassius Clay was on top of the world. He had defeated Sonny Liston, the titan of boxing, without even a scratch on his face. Malcolm X smiled proudly at his friend. While Cassius believed this was all part of Allah's plan, Malcolm knew that this win perfectly fit his own plan, too. Not only did Cassius Clay's dreams come true that night, but Malcolm X also had a feeling his own dreams were about to come true.

Before the match, people had underestimated Cassius and called him a loudmouth. They thought he'd wind up injured in the hospital after facing Sonny. In the end, however, it was Sonny who got a ride to the local hospital and Cassius who went on to his victory party. Cassius headed to the Hampton House, where he had a private celebration with Malcolm X and a few close friends after midnight. His brother, Rudy, singer Sam Cooke, and Jim Brown, the NFL's premier running back, joined them. By the time Cassius arrived, a crowd had already gathered to celebrate his victory. Everyone wanted to shake hands with the new heavyweight champion. Surrounded by a crowd of adoring fans at the Hampton House lunch counter, Cassius ate a huge bowl of ice cream at his victory dinner and smiled for photos. It was one of the happiest moments Cassius Clay and Malcolm X ever shared together. The boxer's win was Malcolm's as well. Friends commented that they seemed as close as brothers.

Later that night, a small group moved into Malcolm's hotel room for a more serious, and private, conversation. Malcolm wanted Cassius to be more active in his plans. It was time for him to share the big picture with his "little brother." Cassius Clay, Malcolm X, and Jim Brown began talking about the future of Black men in America. Jim was also a well-respected professional athlete and understood many of the Nation of Islam's goals. He especially admired Malcolm X. He and Malcolm were both outspoken, demanding rights without apology. Malcolm liked Jim, too. He listened to him and understood that famous Black athletes had a bigger role to play in the freedom movement. Cassius listened, chiming in where he could. The heavyweight title was just the beginning of his accomplishments, which were destined to extend beyond the world of sports and into politics.

Malcolm laid out his plan: Cassius would use his new championship title to serve the movement for Black freedom. As reigning heavyweight titleholder, Cassius had nothing left to conquer in the boxing world. His victories had proven what he believed all along: that he was the greatest. The fighter seemed to support Malcolm's plan. He didn't give any hint that he would change his mind or had other intentions. Yet Cassius went to bed that night, tired from his match, with something on his mind.

The new champ did not sleep long. Maybe it was the excitement of the day or the uneasy feeling he had from his talk with Malcolm that prevented him from resting. When he woke up, Malcolm was gone, but Jim was still in the room. The athletes talked about race in America, the Civil Rights Movement, and the politics of the Nation of Islam. Cassius decided to confide in Jim about his true allegiances. According to Jim, Cassius was sure that Malcolm would never be readmitted into the Nation of Islam. "Elijah was a little man," Brown recalled hearing from Cassius, "but extremely powerful, and had always supported him." As much as Cassius loved Malcolm, their friendship could not go on without incurring the wrath of the Messenger.

CHAPTER NINE

FREEDOM

> I don't have to be what you want me to be.
>
> —*Cassius Clay*

After years in the public eye as the notorious Louisville Lip, Cassius Clay decided it was time to create a new image—one of a more serious world champion. The morning after his championship victory, at a press conference, Cassius explained that he wanted to be a role model for everyone. He even discussed Sonny Liston, admitting that he began to feel sorry for the former champ.

Cassius was like a new man. It seemed he took his

role as heavyweight champion seriously. Before long, reporters began to leave the conference room. One of the remaining writers asked Cassius a question he had been dodging since he first began attending Nation of Islam meetings with Sam Saxon. The reporter asked, "Are you a card-carrying member of the Black Muslims?" Cassius was shocked that anyone would broach that topic. Having just won the heavyweight title, he felt that was the last question they should be concerned about. Also, professional sports involved an unspoken rule for boxers at Cassius's level. They were supposed to avoid politics, religion, or social issues during any media appearances. Standing before television cameras, he'd be forced to answer it honestly.

Talking around the question, Cassius quickly defended the Nation of Islam. He explained that he was not a Christian and attended NOI meetings: "I believe in Allah and in peace." He talked about discipline within his religion, as well as segregation, explaining to white America that he was fine doing things separately. He had no interest in moving to a white neighborhood where he wasn't wanted. After speaking about the many positives within the Nation, Cassius explained that "I don't have to be what you want me to be. I'm free to be who I want."

Reporters watched as Cassius turned into someone else—a serious-minded, vulnerable young man—right before their eyes. Cassius had made it clear that he was no ordinary athlete. Anyone expecting a magnanimous Floyd Patterson or Joe Louis type of boxer after Cassius took home the heavyweight title would be mistaken. Cassius had always spoken his mind, but now his words were bolstered by knowledge and influence. He had learned about history and politics from the ministers in the Nation, and he knew that a powerful Black organization supported him. Malcolm had prepared Cassius for this exact moment—the moment when his fame would become a great platform to address real civil rights issues.

The next morning, Malcolm and Cassius met for breakfast at the Hampton House. Malcolm had read about Elijah Muhammad's recent announcement crediting Cassius's victory to his faith in Allah and inspiration from Elijah. Reading the announcement, Malcolm realized that Elijah was moving closer to Cassius. The Messenger was portraying himself as the most influential person in Cassius's career.

Cassius was trapped between two powerful men at war. He was committed to Elijah and did not know how to navigate his relationship with Malcolm. While Cassius

contemplated this fork in the road, Malcolm realized
that Cassius was not yet committed to his plan. For the
foreseeable future, the minister would have to keep one
eye on Cassius Clay and the other on Elijah Muhammad.

Malcolm and Cassius both regularly talked to the
press about the Nation of Islam. Cassius spent a lot of
his interviews advocating on behalf of Black Muslims
and challenging the media's depiction of the organization
as a hate group or a cult. Beaming with pride, Malcolm
watched as Cassius grew bolder and more confident in his
stance. He had witnessed Cassius mature and felt a deep
connection to this young man he loved like a brother.
The minister rarely trusted anyone, and few ever visited
his home for family dinners the way that Cassius did.
Never did he imagine that Cassius would hurt him. He
trusted his own eyes, seeing only what he wanted to see:
a young Black man eager to learn, full of conviction and
innocence. Unfortunately, Malcolm failed to remember
the key lesson from his relationship with Elijah Muhammad: Things were not always as they seemed.

Later that day, Malcolm X boarded a flight back home
to New York, but his mind remained on the future of
his work with Cassius Clay. The men would be a team.
Malcolm needed Cassius in more ways than one. With

Cassius by his side, he believed Elijah would allow him back in the Nation. Cassius was an influential celebrity who would raise their profile. Malcolm would reconcile with the Messenger by promising to mold Cassius into a leader who could amplify Elijah's message to the world. Alternatively, if he never returned to the Nation, he would need Cassius to help create a new religious movement. Cassius and Malcolm together were unstoppable, and people would join them in droves. Most important, Cassius functioned as an insurance policy for Malcolm. Elijah Muhammad would not attack his former minister as long as Cassius remained friends with him. However, Malcolm would soon realize that Cassius had his own plans.

After Malcolm left for New York, Rudy and Sam arrived in Miami with a message for Cassius. They'd just attended the Saviour's Day convention in Chicago. The Nation did not like the way Malcolm had been clinging to Cassius in Miami. Some leaders were convinced that Malcolm was trying to manipulate Cassius. They confirmed that Malcolm would never be reinstated. In fact, they even hinted that he was a marked man, someone to get rid of by any means necessary. To continue associating with Malcolm, now that he was an enemy of the

Nation of Islam, would be foolish and dangerous. With this new intelligence from the Nation, Cassius had a hard decision to make. No matter the outcome, someone would get hurt.

Cassius decided to take a trip to Malcolm's home base in New York. He and a few of his associates hopped on his personal bus and headed 1,200 miles north. Cassius felt at home as soon as he stepped foot in New York City. He was happy to leave the South. During his long road trip, he experienced the realities of segregation. Although he was the world's heavyweight champion, he was also a Black man in America. That meant that he could not stop at restaurants to eat or use public bathrooms, unless they were designated for Black people. In order to enjoy a decent meal, he often was limited to sandwiches on the bus.

This experience on the road was exactly why Cassius was devoted to the Nation of Islam. As a Black Muslim, he felt empowered by Elijah Muhammad's teachings. He learned that he was great because of the rich history of Black excellence. Being a Black man earned him favor with Allah.

In Harlem, Cassius was in heaven. The streets were filled with Black people greeting him and making him feel special. He was happy to sign autographs and meet with young admirers. He also visited his friend Sam Cooke. The popular musician had come to Cassius's Miami fight, and the two liked to sing together. Sam encouraged Cassius to sing more and even had him record a duet on one of his albums. At once a singer, an actor, a comedian, a poet, and a boxer, Cassius Clay was truly a man of many talents.

Cassius was staying at the historic Hotel Theresa, a Black establishment where Malcolm also resided. After being banished from Temple No. 7, the minister had set up an office there. Malcolm and Cassius met secretly to discuss Malcolm's agenda but were sometimes pictured together around town. Snooping reporters were always interested in the pair's activities. They assumed that Cassius was Malcolm's most devoted follower, and printed news stories declared as much. Reporters thought that Malcolm and Cassius would form their own religious group and take Elijah's followers with them. This was unfounded gossip for the sake of selling newspapers. The media had no idea what Cassius was really going to do, and neither did Malcolm.

Malcolm and Cassius appeared closer than ever. They

toured around New York City, shaking hands with Black residents as though they were on the campaign trail together, running for office. But Malcolm was careful and gave reporters no indication of trying to persuade Cassius to leave the Nation. He even said that Cassius "dances like Sugar Ray, punches like Joe Louis, and thinks like Elijah Muhammad." Malcolm knew that Elijah had people everywhere and didn't want to provoke him any further. Now that the championship match was behind Cassius, Malcolm could soon reveal to him the truth about Elijah Muhammad.

Hundreds of people waited to hear Cassius speak or get an autograph on Broadway in Times Square. It was clear by March 1, 1964, that he was ready to become a leader beyond the world of sports. Malcolm arranged for him to meet a reporter at the *New York Amsterdam News*, a popular Black newspaper. There, Cassius announced that he would no longer acknowledge the name Clay. He explained to the reporter what Elijah and Malcolm had taught him—that his last name was from a "Kentucky slave master," and as such he would no longer use it. Reporters also asked him about the feud between Malcolm and Elijah. Cassius knew better than to comment openly on that, so he pretended there was no feud. He spoke highly of Elijah and talked about Malcolm's great intelligence.

Elijah was increasingly annoyed by how much time the two were spending together. Still, he wasn't sure what he was going to do about it just yet. He knew that Malcolm wanted to return to the Nation, but Elijah didn't trust Malcolm, especially as he moved further and further away from the Messenger's orders. Elijah was convinced that Malcolm was threatening his hold on the members of the Nation. But his own power as the leader of the Nation of Islam was far greater than anything Malcolm could do alone. Elijah fully intended to protect everything he had built and destroy Malcolm.

On March 5, Malcolm brought Cassius with him to the United Nations to meet with delegates from Africa and Asia. Several Black leaders from around the world were in attendance. Malcolm introduced Cassius to African dignitaries and each one expressed their pride in what he had accomplished. Political figures told him how important he was to Black people around the world. At first, Cassius deferred to Malcolm. He was uncomfortable speaking to these foreign politicians about issues

By 1962, Cassius Clay had no doubt that he would become the youngest heavyweight champion in history and the savior of a sport that desperately needed a star. Pictured here at the age of twenty on May 17, 1962.

Minister Malcolm X speaks to a crowd gathered in Harlem, New York, on June 29, 1963.

Cassius Clay, pictured here in 1963, loved admiring himself in the mirror at the 5th Street Gym. "I'm young, I'm handsome, I'm fast, I'm pretty, and can't possibly be beat," he said. "They must fall in the round I call."

Sonny Liston, pictured here in 1964, was the world heavyweight boxing champion from 1962 to 1964, when he lost the title to Cassius Clay.

Cassius Clay in the ring with heavyweight contender Henry Cooper in London, England, in 1963. The Louisville Sponsoring Group sent Clay to Europe in an unsuccessful attempt to create distance between the boxer and Malcolm X.

The Beatles pose for a photo with Cassius Clay at the 5th Street Gym in Miami during their visit to the United States in February 1964.

Cassius Clay lands a punch against defending heavyweight champion Sonny Liston.

"I shook up the world!" Cassius Clay shouted after defeating Sonny Liston to win the heavyweight title. Malcolm X believed Cassius's victory was destiny.

Cassius Clay and Malcolm X celebrate the victory at Hampton House immediately after the boxer defeated Sonny Liston.

Malcolm X and Cassius Clay together in Harlem, New York, during the first week of March 1964.

Left to right: Rudy Clay, Elijah Muhammad, and Cassius Clay. The two brothers became devoted members of the Nation of Islam.

Muhammad Ali draws a crowd in Lagos, Nigeria, during his trip to Africa.

After his trip abroad, Malcolm arrives home to JFK International
Airport in New York on May 21, 1964.

that were unfamiliar. Watching Malcolm X interact with ambassadors, Cassius recognized that Malcolm's relationships could help elevate his own standing on the world stage. Cassius soon relaxed into his new surroundings. Malcolm's plan for Cassius to be more politically engaged was taking shape.

However, Elijah Muhammad was especially angry and jealous when he learned of these meetings at the United Nations. This was the exact type of scenario he feared: Malcolm seducing Cassius into a web of more powerful relationships that excluded him. He also knew that Malcolm was a better speaker than he was. Malcolm had integrity and lived by what he preached to his followers. It would be easy for Malcolm to start his own organization and get people from the Nation to join him—especially if he partnered with Cassius.

Elijah called Cassius after he returned from the UN and immediately gave him instructions. He ordered him to cut ties with Malcolm. It was now or never. Cassius didn't have any more time to think about his choice and ultimately promised Elijah that he would "stop seeing Malcolm starting today." Cassius must have felt torn. He had grown close to Malcolm as a friend, but Elijah was his spiritual leader. Also, Elijah inspired fear. He had loyal followers everywhere, some of whom would not hesitate to hurt anyone he considered an enemy.

If at first Cassius pledged himself to Elijah out of fear, he would soon feel more confident in his decision. As much as he admired Malcolm, he was confused by his behavior. On the day they visited the UN, Malcolm told Cassius and his brother, Rudy, that Elijah was a false prophet, that he had lied to everyone and abused his power. Cassius was stunned. Rudy was so enraged by these claims that he wrestled Malcolm to the floor until Cassius had to pull them apart. The fighter couldn't quite find the logic in this revelation: For two years, Malcolm had drilled into his head that Elijah was a messenger from God. He taught him that Elijah was honorable and the most powerful Black man in America. Now Malcolm expected him to turn his back on a holy man?

Cassius just couldn't understand it. He wondered if Malcolm had been keeping *him* close for a reason other than love and friendship. Despite being the center of attention, Cassius did not let many people get close to him. It was clear that he had two identities: Cassius the boxer and Cassius the Black Muslim. Over the last few years, Cassius had carefully built a wall between himself and the outside world. Sure, he let some people in, but not for long. However, Malcolm was different. The message he shared had made Cassius feel worthy. Now, for maybe the first time, Cassius considered that perhaps Malcolm had just been using him.

It didn't take long for Elijah to think of a way to formalize his grip on Cassius once and for all. On March 6, 1964, Elijah delivered a speech that could be heard on the radio, proclaiming that the name Cassius Clay "has no divine meaning. I hope he will accept being called by a better name. Muhammad Ali is what I will give to him as long as he believes in Allah and follows me." Malcolm heard this broadcast on his car radio and was shocked by Elijah's announcement. "That's political!" he shouted. "That's a political move! He did it to prevent him from coming with me."

Renaming Cassius was considered a great honor in the Nation, and it was Elijah's way of securing the champ's loyalty. Many lifelong members of the Nation never received their original names from Elijah. The champ's Muslim name, Muhammad Ali, meant "worthy of praise," which was fitting for a man who proclaimed he was the greatest.

Malcolm knew that his young friend would have to

make a fateful choice between him and the Messenger. Ultimately, the heavyweight champion submitted to Elijah and became Muhammad Ali. For a man who loved his name, who had shouted it from city to city and even across the ocean, many assumed it would be hard for him to abandon "Cassius Clay." When he first became champion, he had said, "I don't have to be what you want me to be. I'm free to be who I want." But that was not entirely true. As a member of the Nation of Islam, he had to follow orders. He had to end friendships with people that he loved and admired, and he had to mold himself into a different kind of champion, the one the Nation wanted. Elijah Muhammad alone would decide who the boxer could be.

For Malcolm X, this formal name change signaled the end for him. Elijah Muhammad's power and influence were stronger than the bond between Malcolm X and Muhammad Ali. At that point in his life, the boxer was not prepared to become the type of leader Malcolm envisioned him to be. He had mentioned before that he was not interested in protests or political confrontation. Ali felt far more comfortable within the confines of the Nation, where he was endlessly praised simply for being a boxer.

In a panic, Malcolm telephoned Ali after Elijah's announcement, but no one would let him speak to his friend. It was too late. The Black Muslim brothers were already surrounding Muhammad Ali, filtering who could reach him. Without Ali by his side, Malcolm and his family were no longer safe from the Nation. The brothers who had been impatient to hurt Malcolm would not hold back. The threats of violence against him suddenly became very real.

CHAPTER TEN

AMERICA'S NIGHTMARE

America, Africa is watching you.

—*Ghanaian protesters*

America did not like the name "Muhammad Ali." Many thought it sounded too foreign, and people especially didn't like that the name wasn't Christian. Friends and supporters quickly began calling him Ali, but some refused to use his new name. Ali wasn't the first boxer to change his name. Many boxers in the early twentieth century had changed their names to try to assimilate, or fit in, with what they considered "American." They were the sons of immigrants and wanted to make themselves more acceptable to Americans. Even Sonny Liston made fun of the name Muhammad Ali. He pretended he couldn't pronounce it and continued to call him Cassius Clay.

Almost overnight, for many Americans, the popular heavyweight champion became a public disgrace. Recognizing the champ's Muslim name would mean accepting Ali's freedom to define himself, a freedom that many Americans, especially white Americans, were unwilling to honor. Becoming Muhammad Ali meant that he was no longer under the control of sponsors, nor was he bound by the limits of Americans' expectations. Once known as the man who had saved the sport of boxing, Ali was no longer the champion Americans had dreamed of. He was now America's nightmare.

While older Black people disapproved of the Nation of Islam, younger generations saw Ali as a hero. They identified with his self-determination and honesty. Young Black people also respected a man who stood up to authority. The 1960s were one of the most chaotic and tense decades in American history. Young Black people took to the streets and participated in sit-ins in an effort to assert their civil rights. Black youth everywhere were encouraged to demand equal opportunity.

For this generation, Ali represented rebellion, pride, and defiance. He refused to be perceived as the "good," agreeable Black man or someone hoping for white people to show him respect. He commanded respect effortlessly—which at the time was an amazing power.

Now that Ali had earned the heavyweight title, sportswriters and politicians resumed their campaign to eliminate boxing. They did not want a Black Muslim champion. Some demanded an investigation into the championship fight. The betting odds going into the fight so heavily favored Liston, they didn't believe Ali won fairly. It soon became clear that there was no evidence of foul play. Ali had won fair and square. But that didn't stop critics. The World Boxing Association threatened to take away Ali's title because they believed he was bad for boxing and a bad example for children across the world.

Officials, critics, and angry fans wanted to punish Ali for joining the Nation of Islam. Many Black Americans were also upset. They thought that Ali did not represent their best interests. He had spoken out against integration before and had turned his nose up at the thought of protesting for racial equality; but now in the Nation of Islam, he had officially joined forces against civil rights activists. For that, he could not be forgiven. Ali was an outcast for both rejecting his Christian name and rejecting the Civil Rights Movement.

In New York, Malcolm X was living his own nightmare. Elijah Muhammad had launched an all-out war against him. He branded Malcolm a hypocrite—which to Black Muslims was the worst kind of person. Hypocrites were people who falsely presented themselves as followers of Allah and his Messenger. Elijah Muhammad had members of the Fruit of Islam follow Malcolm, harass him, and even threaten his safety. Malcolm knew his life was in danger and accepted that he might die soon.

However, he did not let the Nation stop him from trying to fight for Black people. Malcolm had to let the world know that he was a different man, free to act on his own convictions. Now that he was no longer under Elijah's control, Malcolm promised to join the fight for civil rights. He said that he'd help anywhere he could. Malcolm planned to create his own Black political organization. He laid out his plans to organize a voting campaign, speak at colleges, and work with southern civil rights groups. Years before, he had spoken out against these groups on behalf of the Nation, but now he was free to support them. Malcolm also made it clear that he would not try to lure away any of Muhammad's followers. When reporters asked, he told them that members of the NOI should continue to follow Elijah, just to keep the peace.

But Elijah still wanted to destroy him. He sent his captains to take back everything that belonged to the Nation of Islam—including the home Malcolm and his family lived in. Malcolm was furious. He had worked hard for the Nation and taken a vow of poverty, deciding that any money he earned would go to Elijah Muhammad. Malcolm didn't own any property and didn't have any money. Even the profits from the book he was writing with Alex Haley belonged to the Nation. Malcolm regretted ever taking a vow of poverty, but it was too late. He had to work even harder to get his new organization—Muslim Mosque, Inc.—off the ground.

Malcolm could command a crowd, and journalists were always interested in what he had to say. By March 1964, he began promoting MMI as a politically oriented Black Nationalist group of Muslims and non-religious people. This new Malcolm, who distanced himself from Elijah Muhammad, was likable. Many reporters who, in the past, had described him as violent now saw a different side of him. "It is almost impossible, upon meeting him, not to like him," said journalist Dick Schaap. The media soon realized that they'd never really known Malcolm. Under Elijah's control, he was never able to show his full power and capabilities.

Many reporters and fans were excited to see what a free Malcolm would accomplish in this new chapter of his career. At the Cory Methodist Church in Cleveland, Ohio, following his split from the NOI, Malcolm said: "We need to expand the civil rights struggle to a higher level—to the level of human rights." Focusing on civil rights made Black Americans too dependent on the US government, which had already failed to protect their legal rights. "I am not an American," he declared. "I am one of twenty-two million black people who are the victims of Americanism."

By all accounts, most reporters figured the friendship between Malcolm X and Muhammad Ali was over. However, Ali was staying in the same Harlem building where Malcolm worked. The two must have run into each other a few times, or even had a friendly conversation. In fact, one reporter mentioned that Ali had come into Malcolm's office in late March 1964 for a private conversation. It was clear that the two were not supposed to be seen together. Malcolm told a reporter, "We are brothers, and we have much in common." Ali, however, would not say the same, for fear of upsetting Elijah Muhammad. As the violent rhetoric against Malcolm increased, the fighter began to distance himself even more from Malcolm. He knew that members of the Nation would turn on him, too, if he said anything that resembled a kind statement about the former minister.

Malcolm soon began planning a trip to Africa and southwest Asia, where he would visit many countries, including Egypt, Nigeria, Ghana, and Saudi Arabia. He wanted to expand his understanding of Islam and renew his faith. At this time, Malcolm was under a lot of stress. He was ousted from the Nation of Islam, had lost a father figure in Elijah Muhammad, and risked losing his housing—if the Nation had its way. On top of that, he lived in constant fear for his life.

He thought this was a good time to make the pilgrimage to Mecca, the holiest Muslim city in the world. Muslims are called to take a trip to Mecca, to complete their hajj, at least once in their lifetime as an important part of their religious practice. Muslims believe that making the hajj pilgrimage to Mecca deepens one's faith and offers a chance for cleansing past sins before Allah. Before his travels, Malcolm continued promoting his new organization around the United States and preached that Black people needed to be in control of their own communities, politics, and religion. He also advised Black people to practice self-defense and work together in the struggle against injustice and police brutality. He emphasized that Black people were "African-Americans... Africans born in America." Each of these points defined his Black Nationalist agenda.

Malcolm had inspired Muhammad Ali to travel to Africa as well, an idea first born out of their meetings with African dignitaries at the United Nations. African leaders had praised the boxer as an international hero. When he changed his name and announced he was a Muslim, his American supporters quickly turned on him. They called him "un-American." As the hateful comments grew louder, Ali soon began to understand what Malcolm was talking about: He was only an American if he did what those in power wanted him to do. He finally understood what Malcolm meant when he said that they were Africans born in America. It was time for Ali to discover another dimension of himself.

"The king! The king!" the crowd yelled as Muhammad Ali rode by in a cream-colored convertible in May 1964.

He had made it to Accra, Ghana, the first stop in a five-week trip. The locals loved him. Ghanaians treated him like royalty, and Ali loved every minute of it. He was surprised to see that this part of the world was not at all how Americans had described it. Driving through Ghana, he saw streetlights, public transportation systems, modern apartment buildings, and stores. There were nice hotels and restaurants where Black and white people sat together. American television and movies had led him to believe that all of Africa was a vast jungle inhabited by dangerous, wild animals. But Ghana was nothing like the American media's depictions. It was beautiful.

Ali toured Accra and spoke to reporters. He advised that Black people should move to Africa if America refused to give them justice. Elijah was pleased with Ali's words. He knew the champion could bring positive global attention to the Nation of Islam. Elijah Muhammad wanted the world to think of the NOI as important global leaders dedicated to helping Black people everywhere. But this was very far from the truth. Elijah had traveled Africa before and was very condescending and judgmental. He did not really want to build any relationships with African nations. Instead, he wanted boost his own profile on the world stage.

Seeing that Elijah was being deceitful, Malcolm X spoke out. He knew that Elijah was using Ali for personal gain. The more popular Ali became, the more attention the Nation received, and the more donations rolled in to Elijah's bank account. Instead of viciously attacking Elijah, Malcolm simply presented the facts, explaining: "You cannot read anything that Elijah Muhammad has ever written that's pro-African." Indeed, no one could find such words. Still, Elijah's followers ignored the truth. No matter what Malcolm said, they would not see Elijah as anything other than a holy man.

Elijah Muhammad had predicted that the heavyweight champion would receive a hero's welcome during his trip abroad and that it would boost the Messenger's mission in the United States. Muhammad was right. In Ghana, Ali realized he was more popular in Africa than at home. Most Americans refused to stop calling him Cassius Clay. But in Ghana, Nigeria, and Egypt, people showed him respect. They addressed him as Muhammad Ali and treated him as if he were their own national champion.

As Ali spent more time abroad, he began to change. He knew he had purpose in this world, but being around so many people who looked like him and respected him shaped how he viewed himself and his life in America. This trip was when Cassius Clay really became Muhammad Ali.

About a week before Ali arrived in Accra, another famous Black American arrived: Malcolm X. During his travels across Africa, one of Malcolm's hosts took him to a local boxing match, where Malcolm discovered how popular the sport was there. Because he had been photographed with Muhammad Ali so much, some locals thought he actually *was* Ali. He soon began sharing pictures and telling stories of the great heavyweight champ. In doing so, he gained many new Muslim friends wherever he went. But Malcolm was not the same man he'd been in the pictures with Ali. Those images represented Malcolm X, Nation of Islam minister, and Cassius Clay, a boxer on the rise. Now things had changed. Malcolm and Ali had changed.

The former minister needed to complete his pilgrimage to Mecca, so that he could refocus and reclaim his identity. Malcolm, like Ali, needed his spirituality to ground him. When he came back from his hajj, he understood that Islam was not just a Black man's religion, as Elijah had taught him. He saw people from all over the world praying together. It didn't matter if they were white, brown, or Black; they all came together as devoted Muslims. Malcolm rededicated himself to Islam and upholding the holy book, the Quran. He renamed himself El-Hajj Malik el-Shabazz, but in America he would still go by Malcolm X.

Malcolm knew now that everything Elijah taught him about Islam was against the Quran. He also felt that it might be possible for Black and white people to live together peacefully, though he had his doubts that this was possible in the United States. As a member of the Nation, he had believed that all white people were devils. But performing the hajj cleansed him of this belief. Finally, after visiting Mecca, Malcolm accepted that Elijah Muhammad was not the messenger of Allah and that the true power of Islam was not in separating people but in bringing them together.

Near the end of his trip, Malcolm arrived in Accra, Ghana, where he planned to meet with Ghanaian president Kwame Nkrumah and several Black Americans who had relocated there. Accra, Ghana, had long been a popular place for Black American expatriates and thought leaders such as W. E. B. Du Bois, Richard Wright, and Maya Angelou. Ghanaians also kept up with American news as the civil rights protests and anti-Black violence were broadcast in Ghana. After the March on Washington in 1963, a small group of Ghanaian protesters demonstrated outside the American embassy. They carried signs that read, AMERICA, AFRICA IS WATCHING YOU.

President Nkrumah was well aware of how America mistreated Black people, but he didn't want to upset the American government, which had the power to send financial and military aid to his country. Under these circumstances, Nkrumah was careful not to seem too friendly with Malcolm when they met. Malcolm wanted President Nkrumah to advance a United Nations resolution—or rule—that would charge the United States with human rights violations for failing to protect Black Americans. After hearing him out, President Nkrumah declined. He could not risk offending the US government. Malcolm was disappointed but he understood that going against the United States was no small request.

Malcolm continued to pursue relationships with other African leaders. His travels had deepened his commitment to the shared world struggle against racial injustice. He declared, "Our problems were their problems. We are all one people—Africans or of African descent. We are all blood brothers!"

On May 17, 1964, Malcolm prepared to leave Ghana

to complete the second half of his trip. He still wanted to visit Senegal and North African countries. He and his friends stood at the front of the Ambassador Hotel, packing his luggage into a car. Suddenly the sound of American English caught their attention. One voice was very familiar: Muhammad Ali's. It felt as if time had frozen. Malcolm had not expected to see Ali in Accra. Malcolm broke the silence by shouting to his old friend, "Brother Muhammad!" He half smiled, uncertain if Ali would be happy to see him. As soon as Ali heard Malcolm's voice, he turned, encircled by men from the Nation of Islam.

At this moment, Ali had to be careful how he reacted because it would surely be reported back to Elijah Muhammad. Ali paused and looked at Malcolm, who appeared much different than the last time they'd met. Malcolm now had a reddish goatee to match his famous red-tinted hair. He wore a white robe and sandals. This was nothing like the black suits and ties he wore in Harlem. At first, Ali didn't respond to Malcolm. He kept walking, slowly moving away from Malcolm and his group. But the former minister wouldn't let his friend leave without a word. He tried to flag him down as Ali and his entourage moved toward a car.

Finally, the fighter faced him. Before anyone could

intervene, Malcolm said, "Brother, I still love you, and you are still the greatest." Ali did not tell Malcolm that he still loved him, too. Perhaps he was afraid to care openly about Malcolm in front of Nation of Islam members. Maybe he believed the lies Elijah spread about Malcolm being a hypocrite. It's impossible to know what Ali truly felt at that moment. But he turned his back on Malcolm. "You left the Honorable Elijah Muhammad," he said in response. "That was the wrong thing to do."

Malcolm knew that Elijah had portrayed him as a traitor to the Nation of Islam. But he didn't leave the Nation by choice, he was kicked out. Elijah made it seem that stealing followers to form a competing organization had always been Malcolm's big plan. Many people believed Elijah's lies, but Malcolm never thought that his brother Ali would.

After this painful encounter, Malcolm retreated. His friend Maya Angelou drove him to the airport for the next leg of his trip, and the mood in the car was somber. This brief encounter between the two men would change their lives forever. Seeing Malcolm physically changed— dressed in a robe with long facial hair—had somehow convinced Ali that Elijah's criticisms of the former minister were true. Ali didn't realize that Malcolm, newly returned from his hajj, was wearing traditional Muslim attire. He judged Malcolm just as many Americans judged him—unfairly. After walking away from Malcolm, Ali turned to Herbert Muhammad, Elijah's son, and said, "Man, did you get a look at him? Dressed in that funny white robe and wearing a beard and walking with that cane that looked like a prophet's stick?...He's gone so far out he's out completely." Ali hardly recognized Malcolm. "Doesn't that just go to show, Herbert, that Elijah is the most powerful? Nobody listens to that Malcolm anymore."

Both men had changed, and it was clear that they were on different, dangerous paths. Ali was Elijah's servant, placing all his hopes and dreams in a false prophet pretending to be a holy man. Just as Elijah had done, Ali turned his back on someone he once loved. And Malcolm, now an outcast, had angered a man who commanded an army that would easily resort to violence upon request. Malcolm X and Muhammad Ali were brothers, torn apart by a jealous leader. Their encounter in Accra would be the very last time they met.

Yet Malcolm still cared for Ali and could not help but try to protect him. Before departing Accra, he sent Ali a telegram, offering brotherly advice as he always did, reminding him of his immense influence with people all around the world. Malcolm wrote:

> Because a billion of our people in Africa, Arabia, and Asia love you blindly, you must now be forever aware of your tremendous responsibilities to them. You must never say or do anything that will permit your enemies to distort the beautiful image you have here among our people.

When Malcolm made a vague reference to Ali's "enemies," he was really talking about his own rivals in the Nation of Islam, those dangerous men who would use Ali and discard him when he was no longer valuable, just as they did to Malcolm.

CHAPTER ELEVEN

BY ANY MEANS NECESSARY

He got what he deserved.

—*Muhammad Ali*

On May 21, 1964, Malcolm returned home from Africa and found himself at a crossroads between his future and his past. His political outlook had evolved greatly from his previous beliefs. Whereas he once spoke harshly against white people, he now considered some of them his allies, as long as they recognized the humanity of Black people. He now aimed to work with people from different races and religions. Malcolm had great, big ideas but struggled to find the right path to accomplish them.

"Separation is not the goal of the Afro-American," he told a moderator during a public debate. "Nor is integration [the] goal. They are merely methods towards [the] real end—respect and recognition as a human being."

Another pressing issue affecting Malcolm's activism was that he didn't have funding to build a political movement. Organizing revolutionary movements and traveling across the world took money. The Nation of Islam was still trying to seize the home he lived in, and any earnings he made now were split between his growing family and his organization, Muslim Mosque, Inc. Still, Malcolm never gave up the fight. Brotherhood between Black people across the globe would be his main focus going forward. He considered anyone who decided to fight beside him his brother.

Now that Malcolm was settled back in Harlem, the Nation began harassing him again. Members would appear in groups at his rallies, interviews, and even his house. The Nation's security team, the Fruit of Islam, had been ordered to hurt Malcolm. They sent him death threats and told anyone who would listen that Malcolm would not survive much longer. Malcolm sensed that the Fruit of Islam were closing in on him, walking around his neighborhood or in cars parked outside his home. He was on high alert, watching every shadow and listening for any strange footsteps behind him.

The bullies had pushed Malcolm into a corner and the only way to get out was to fight back. Malcolm's most powerful weapon? The truth. He went on TV and radio stations to share Elijah Muhammad's transgressions. He secured proof that Elijah had several secret families. He revealed how ruthless Elijah could be with members of the Nation who stepped out of line. On June 7, 1964, at an event in Harlem, Malcolm told a crowd of five hundred about Elijah's tactics. The audience was shocked to learn that Malcolm had obtained signed legal documents from women who claimed that Elijah was the father of their children.

The next day, Malcolm received several alarming phone calls, presumably from members of the NOI. They threatened his wife, Betty, and even his young daughters. Still, Malcolm refused to back down. He thought that publicizing his death threats would give him added protection from assassins, but it also scared away potential members from attending his meetings.

With Malcolm out of the picture, Muhammad Ali became the Nation of Islam's favored member. He preached before larger crowds of Black Muslims whenever Elijah asked him. He talked about how the wise Messenger had changed his life. It was everything Elijah wanted. As a collective, the Nation continued to bash Malcolm's character at every turn, calling him a hypocrite and a traitor. Elijah encouraged his members to punish Malcolm and even allowed *Muhammad Speaks*, the organization's newspaper, to print negative images and stories about him. The smear campaign against Malcolm created a hostile environment of bloodthirsty men ready for revenge. Elijah Muhammad and his captains generated a frenzy that was sure to end in violence.

But some NOI members opposed the ruthless persecution of Malcolm. Some Black Muslims who had known the former minister thought Elijah's leadership was getting too violent. It was one thing to criticize someone's actions, but quite another to say that such an individual deserved to die. One of Elijah's grandsons even left the Nation in light of this troubling turn, calling his grandfather a fraud. He said that Elijah stole from the poor and that NOI leadership took advantage of people. Wallace, Elijah's son, agreed with his nephew. He knew he couldn't redirect the Nation of Islam's values or priorities overnight, but he hoped that one day he'd be in a position to make significant change.

While Ali was riding the wave of popularity within the Nation of Islam, he met a young woman, Sonji Roi, and they got married quickly. Sonji was not a Muslim but agreed to follow some of the Nation's rules. As a newly-wed enjoying his homelife, Ali stopped training. Angelo Dundee worried that the champ was losing interest in boxing. Ali was out of shape, but still signed a contract for a rematch with Sonny Liston in Boston. Ali didn't think much of the fight, but he wanted to prove once and for all that his heavyweight victory was well earned. Another win, this time by knockout, would silence his critics for good.

After months of training, Ali arrived in Boston like a new man. He was ready for the rematch, scheduled for late November 1964. However, the much-anticipated showdown would have to wait. Just a few days before the fight, Ali was rushed to the emergency room with a terrible stomachache. Doctors discovered that he had a hernia, a large swelling inside his stomach that required immediate surgery. He wouldn't be able to fight for several months.

Back in New York, Malcolm couldn't shake the feeling that his life would soon end. He'd recently gone on a five-month trip touring Africa for a second time that year, meeting with a few leaders and his old friends in Accra. Malcolm's friends abroad could see that he was deeply troubled. He'd told them that he had traveled away from home even longer because, back in Harlem, men were out to get him. Malcolm was right.

Elijah had issued another message to his followers saying that Malcolm's time was almost up. Men from the Nation couldn't wait for him to come back to Harlem so they could carry out Elijah's orders. Even his old friend Louis X threatened violence as soon as Malcolm stepped back in Harlem. Although Malcolm woke up every day wondering if it might be his last, his greatest fear was abandoning the fight for Black freedom.

He had so much work to do and it was clear that his time was running out. In December 1964, he called a reporter from the *New York Post* for an urgent meeting. He wanted to get his thoughts on the public record. He said that he was "for the freedom of the 22 million Afro-Americans by *any means necessary.*" He was on edge, desperate to see immediate results. Near the end of the interview, Malcolm talked about his life and what he was willing to sacrifice for freedom. Malcolm wanted people to know the truth about what he fought for. He wanted people to know that through it all, he was for the freedom of Black Americans. It was clear that Malcolm thought this interview might be his last.

That winter the cold temperatures arrived just as Malcolm and his associates were being frozen out by the NOI. One of Malcolm's friends, Leon Ameer, was attacked in his hotel room. He had tried to warn Muhammad Ali that Elijah was just using him. The Nation responded by beating Ameer nearly to death. Once he recovered, he told reporters that the Nation of Islam was dangerous and would hurt anyone who supported Malcolm. He also claimed that Ali was in danger.

Reporters quickly asked Ali to respond to Leon's claims. Everyone was surprised by his cruel statement, "[Leon] got what he deserved." The media was shocked that a once-charming young man had turned so cold and distant. More than ever, Ali sounded like the brutal men he spent time with. He even claimed that anyone who went against Elijah Muhammad "[knows] they deserve to be killed for what they did." Ali echoed his mentor, unknowingly becoming a puppet who would be used in the assassination plot against Malcolm X. The fighter was the most popular voice in the Nation. His words mattered. Just as with Elijah, when he said someone deserved to die, people took him seriously. Ali's words supported acts of violence against Malcolm X.

Malcolm began to wonder just how many people wanted him gone. He knew the Nation of Islam was his enemy but began to notice strange things that pointed to another threatening group: the FBI. In late January 1965, Malcolm flew to Los Angeles for business. When he arrived at his hotel, he noticed several members of the Fruit of Islam in the lobby. One man in particular, John Ali, caught his attention. John was a high-ranking member of the Nation. But Malcolm had always suspected he was secretly an informant for the FBI. He was sure that John was one of the people who would spy on him and report back to the FBI. How else could the Fruit of Islam have known exactly what flight he'd be on? Or which hotel he'd be staying at in Los Angeles? He had told only his closest, most trustworthy allies about this trip. The FBI would be the only other source capable of knowing this information.

The hotel run-in was just the beginning of more aggressive threats against Malcolm. On his way to the Los Angeles airport, traveling next to Chicago, Malcolm was chased through traffic by two cars, and inside the airport, LA police intercepted two more Nation members.

In Chicago, Malcolm was under heavy police protection. He left an interview in an unmarked police car with two detectives and two attorneys by his side. Suddenly a van swerved in front of them, cutting off the police car. A dozen attackers swarmed their vehicle. Fortunately, six officers arrived to help. When Malcolm got to his hotel, he recognized fifteen Nation members in the lobby. Malcolm felt defeated. "It's only going to be a matter of time before they catch up with me," he told a detective.

Under all this stress, Malcolm was compelled to head south and join the grassroots civil rights activists. By that time, Malcolm had created the Organization of Afro-American Unity (OAAU), a movement inspired by his trip to Africa and the limitations of Muslim Mosque, Inc. He recognized that Muslim Mosque, Inc., turned off too many non-Muslims who wished to join him in the Black freedom struggle. So he courted Black intellectuals and activists to join him in OAAU, a group that would pursue voter registration drives, boycotts against racist business owners, and "an all-out war on organized crime."

When he arrived in Selma, Alabama, in early February 1965, Martin Luther King Jr. had just been arrested for leading a march for voting rights. He was jailed along with a startling seven hundred other protesters. Activists from the Student Nonviolent Coordinating Committee invited Malcolm to speak at a rally. Malcolm accepted and praised King's commitment to nonviolence. He made sure to let listeners know that his methods were different from King's, but he respected him. Listening to Malcolm speak, some may have hoped that he and King would eventually work together, combining two powerful visions to push for equal rights. While King was in jail, Malcolm visited the reverend's wife, Coretta. He wasn't able to visit King, but Malcolm wanted Coretta to let him know that he was available for support.

Following his travels to Africa the year before, Malcolm declared, "We are all one people—Africans or of African descent," and his actions supported that allyship. After visiting Alabama, Malcolm flew to London for the first Congress of the Council of African Organizations— an event that reflected his newfound commitment to the international struggle against racial injustice. A few days later, on February 9, Malcolm arrived in Paris. However, the French authorities detained him as soon as he stepped off the plane. Someone had tipped them off that he was coming—and that he was trouble. They claimed he threatened to disturb "the public order." The French authorities made it clear to Malcolm that he was not welcome in France. He was sent right back to London.

Malcolm was neither a criminal nor a wanted man. He had visited France just three months earlier, with no issues. Malcolm recognized that the United States government had enough power to tarnish his relationship with France. He was aware that the FBI had been following him, but it was now clear that several other American organizations, like the Central Intelligence Agency, had been tracking him, too. Malcolm knew the Nation of Islam wanted him dead, but now, after witnessing how quickly he was expelled from France, he questioned which organization was most desperate to eliminate him—the U.S. government, or the Nation of Islam—and which would get to him first.

Finally, on February 13, Malcolm returned home to New York. That night he could not get any rest. He felt uneasy and it took him a long time to fall asleep. At 2:45 AM, Malcolm woke up to the sound of a window breaking in the living room. Before he could understand what was happening, fire was everywhere. His anxious instincts were right: A firebomb had shattered the window and crashed into the living room floor, setting everything ablaze. Suddenly, a second firebomb crashed through another window.

Malcolm shook Betty awake and rushed into the next room to get their four daughters. Smoke filled the girls' room as Malcolm picked them up, all screaming. Betty crossed the hallway, making her way through smoke and avoiding glass on the floor. Malcolm found Betty and guided her and the girls to the backyard. Knowing they were now safe, Malcolm rushed back inside, through the fire, to get something. Betty watched their home burn down as she and the children stood in the snow, barefoot, in freezing temperatures.

Malcolm returned with coats and a weapon for protection. He didn't know if the attackers would double back and try to harm his wife and children. Malcolm must have thought about his childhood in Lansing, Michigan, where his home was burned down. Back then, the perpetrators were white supremacists cloaked in white sheets. But on this night in Queens, New York, as Malcolm comforted his wife and children, it was clear that this violent attack was carried out by men he'd once called brothers.

The local fire department arrived within five minutes. Malcolm was furious—the Nation of Islam had gone too far. What if one of his daughters had died in the fire? What if Betty had been trapped in the burning house? His youngest daughter was just seven months old. He would never expect his enemies to be so atrocious. In the days after the fire, the Nation denied any involvement. Some people dared to claim that Malcolm started the fire himself.

Ali even went on TV to discredit Malcolm. He said that Malcolm was a liar and no one should take him seriously. It was a terrible thing to say about a man who had taught him so much. Betty didn't like this behavior at all. She confronted Ali the next time she saw him. But Ali deflected her. "I haven't done anything," he said. "I'm not doing anything to him." Even though Muhammad Ali would never bomb someone's home, he was guilty of inciting violence against Malcolm, and now Malcolm's family.

Two days after the attack on his home, Malcolm struck back against the NOI, revealing that Elijah Muhammad entertained negotiations with the violent white supremacist organization the Ku Klux Klan. Elijah never criticized or challenged the Klan, precisely because they had made an agreement to keep the peace on the land the Messenger wanted to buy in the South. With this revelation, Malcolm hoped to discredit Elijah for good. Surely,

Elijah's followers would wonder how the Messenger could have cooperated with a group of white supremacists who terrorized Black people.

Despite the repeated attempts on his life, Malcolm continued traveling the country and growing his organization. He realized he could not build a movement if people were too scared to gather. "We don't want people feeling uneasy," he said to his security team. "We must create an image that makes people feel at home." Each person who entered the rally on February 15 was patted down, and Malcolm had guards standing around the building. He instructed his security to stop frisking people in an effort to make them feel safer.

With the relaxed measures, Malcolm was at higher risk than before. He never really had enough security to begin with, and now it would be easier for someone to bring a weapon into one of his events. Malcolm knew that his enemies in the NOI followed his every move, and the FBI still had his phone tapped. What he didn't know was that Gene Roberts, Malcolm's head of security, was also an NYPD detective, planted undercover among Malcolm's support staff. It was possible that the FBI had also planted an informant amid his own camp of followers.

If they could infiltrate the Nation of Islam, he was sure they could also have a mole in his inner circle. Malcolm was suspicious, but he never pinpointed exactly who the culprits were. Wherever Malcolm went and whatever he said, he knew his enemies were close behind.

During a photo shoot for *Life* magazine, Malcolm restated that he was in danger. He explained that his enemies had tried twice to end his life in a span of two weeks. When the photographer suggested the police could help him, Malcolm chuckled and said, "Nobody can protect you from a Muslim but a Muslim—or someone trained in Muslim tactics." Malcolm knew he was not protected; there was not much he could do to prevent whatever would happen to him. He added, "Oh, there are hunters and there are those who hunt the hunters. But the odds are certainly with those who are most skilled at the game."

Just a few days after Malcolm and his family were nearly killed in a house fire, he was preparing to speak in front of a crowd at the Audubon Ballroom in the Manhattan neighborhood of Washington Heights, a place he had visited many times before. Less than twenty-four hours before Malcolm's event, a man named Talmadge X and his associates attended a dance at the Audubon Ballroom, where they were able to inspect the venue's windows and exits, finalizing their plans to kill the minister.

For years, Malcolm had been speaking in front of large crowds; it was second nature to him. But something about that day—February 21, 1965—felt wrong. That morning he'd woken up to a call from a mysterious man who simply said, "Wake up, brother" and hung up. He had asked Betty to bring the girls to the rally, something he had previously stopped doing for fear of his family's safety. The New York City Police Department, which usually had four or five officers guarding the entrance of the Audubon, posted only one police officer that day—despite Roberts's urgent warnings to his supervisors about the rising death threats from the Nation of Islam. Strangely, the NYPD had instead stationed nearly twenty policemen to the hospital across the street from the Audubon, a safe distance away from this politically charged event. Meanwhile, Malcolm's guest speaker was nowhere to be found and no one had printed the official program outlining his speech. Malcolm was tense and tired. He admitted to his assistants, "I feel that I should not be here. Something is wrong, brothers."

Talmadge X and his four accomplices parked a few

blocks away from the Audubon. They scouted the building's perimeter and concealed their weapons under long, heavy coats. They knew that Malcolm had reduced security at previous meetings and had stopped frisking guests. The men made sure to find seats by the stage, just like they'd planned, each of them with a gun under his coat. Their getaway driver sat in the middle of the four-hundred-person crowd. While many had come to hear a message of empowerment, Talmadge and his brothers sought something far more sinister.

Without a guest speaker or official program, Malcolm's friend Benjamin had to give the introduction. He spoke for twenty minutes before introducing Malcolm. Malcolm slowly took the stage wearing a dark brown suit. His signature smile was missing. The audience gave him a standing ovation. Looking at the crowd, Malcolm cracked a half smile to acknowledge his appreciation for their enthusiasm. Right before he began, Roberts walked toward the back of the ballroom, leaving only two bodyguards near Malcolm. When the audience finally quieted down, he greeted them, "As-salaam-alaikum." They crowd responded "Wa-alaikum-salaam." It was a call-and-response his followers had come to look forward to, signaling peace and well-wishes.

Malcolm took a long breath and began, "Brothers and sisters...," but a disturbance in the crowd stopped him midsentence. A man jumped up from his seat, tossed a homemade smoke bomb, and shouted, "Get your hand out of my pocket!" It was the exact same phrase heard during another tense commotion among Malcolm's followers a few days earlier. Two men seemed to be fighting. Some in the audience began yelling, causing even more confusion. The chaos got the attention of Malcolm's two remaining guards, who had been stationed near him. They went to break up the fight, leaving Malcolm alone and exposed on the stage. "Now, now brothers," Malcolm urged, "break it up. Be cool..." Malcolm tried to calm things down, just as he'd done a few days earlier. However, Malcolm's enemies were no longer in practice mode. This time, their plan to assassinate Malcolm was underway.

Suddenly, another man stepped into the aisle. "Hold it!" Malcolm said, extending his arm in the air. Betty and his children were in the front row. A loud *boom!* erupted and everyone began screaming and running toward the exit. By the time anyone understood what was happening, Malcolm X was on the floor, injured by several gunshot wounds. Betty, pregnant at the time with twins, desperately tried to cover her girls, shielding them from the horror of seeing their father's death.

Only one of the shooters, Talmadge X, was caught by Malcolm's guards. Malcolm's followers held him down and beat him until the police came and took him away. Betty kneeled beside her husband. She frantically tried to save his life, but nothing could be done. Malcolm's heart had stopped beating. Betty, Malcolm's guards, his daughters, and his followers cried together. The sound of heartbreak filled the ballroom and slowly moved into the streets of Harlem.

February 21, 1965, would forever be known as the day that Malcolm X was assassinated. Three of Malcolm's young daughters and his pregnant wife witnessed his murder. It was a devastating time for Malcolm's family and his followers, all of whom were furious. They believed the Nation was responsible for Malcolm's death and promised to avenge their leader. Although one suspect was arrested, Malcolm's assassination created more questions than answers: Why weren't the spectators searched? Why wasn't there tighter security near the stage? Why was the NYPD so heavily stationed at the hospital? Was this an inside job? Malcolm had told his most trusted assistants that the FBI had agents working inside the Nation. He knew that those informants had fueled the conflict between himself and Elijah Muhammad, intending to spark mutually assured destruction between two powerful Black American men. Malcolm's circle didn't doubt that Talmadge X acted on behalf of the Nation of Islam, but the question most people wanted addressed was: Who sent the assassins?

Elijah Muhammad denied any involvement in the assassination and denied knowing the killers, but Malcolm's followers did not believe him. They threatened him and Muhammad Ali. The threats were so bad that Ali's mother publicly said that she hoped her son would leave the Nation for good. She sensed that her son was troubled and assumed Ali was thinking about quitting the Nation. However, she knew that leaving Elijah was more dangerous than staying with him—despite the threats from Malcolm's followers.

On the bitterly cold day of Malcolm's funeral, a few thousand people lined the streets of Harlem to mourn him. Earlier in the week, inside a Christian church, twenty thousand people paid their respects to Malcolm as he lay in a copper-colored casket. At the Faith Temple Church of God in Christ on Amsterdam Avenue, Betty and Malcolm's friends made sure that the service was done in traditional Muslim fashion. Ossie Davis, a great actor and friend to Malcolm, gave a powerful eulogy. The eulogy honored Malcolm and spoke of all the good he had done. He called Malcolm one of Harlem's "brightest hopes," adding, "In honoring him, we honor the best in ourselves."

At the Ferncliff Cemetery in Westchester County, New York, a plaque with Malcolm's chosen Muslim name, El-Hajj Malik el-Shabazz, marked the fearless leader's final resting place. His death affected people around the world. Some of the most notable civil rights leaders, including Bayard Rustin and John Lewis, attended his funeral. Ali, who had loved Malcolm as a brother, did not attend. He could not have, even if he wanted to be there. Elijah made sure to forbid his followers from attending the funeral of a hypocrite.

Ali carried on with his boxing career and his personal life as though Malcolm's death didn't affect him. People wondered if Ali ever loved Malcolm at all. How could he go on laughing and clowning when his brother was so gruesomely murdered? He couldn't show remorse for Malcolm's murder, and maybe Ali's greatest performance was pretending that it didn't scare or hurt him at all. He would continue to surround himself with the violent men who were responsible for Malcolm's demise. The men were dangerous fanatics who were capable of anything, including killing a beloved leader in broad daylight. Malcolm's life was over, but his words lived on. His hopes and dreams for Black freedom across the world would be ignited each time Black people demanded justice, each time Black people spoke truth to power, and each time someone was reminded that Black rights matter.

EPILOGUE

ONCE THE HATE IS GONE

The athlete of the decade has to be Cassius
Clay, who is now Muhammad Ali. He is
all that the sixties were. It is as though he
were created to represent them.

—*Jimmy Cannon,*
sportswriter, 1970

In the months following Malcolm's death, Ali went on pretending the assassination didn't affect him. Malcolm's followers had not forgiven him for turning against his brother. Rumors circulated that hundreds of armed men were heading Ali's way. There were so many threats against him that Ali might have considered training in a bulletproof vest. As the big rematch with Sonny Liston got closer, fans were afraid to attend for fear that a bomb or poison gas would disrupt the fight. All the talk about possible violence caused the fight to be moved from Boston, Massachusetts, to Lewiston, Maine, a much smaller town with fewer ticket sales.

Finally, on May 25, 1965, the historic rematch was underway. After the opening bell rang, Ali marched toward Liston, hitting him hard. They danced around the ring for a minute before Sonny lost his balance. Just then, Ali snuck a quick punch that landed right on Sonny's chin. Sonny collapsed to the floor, sinking the last of his reputation with him. The crowd immediately booed. They screamed that the fight had to be a fake. No one could believe that Ali's one punch could knock a big, strong man like Sonny Liston down hard enough to end the fight. This time, cameras were able to do a slow-motion playback. It showed, without a doubt, that Ali had punched Sonny, causing him to fall down. Now there wasn't anyone who could claim that Ali was anything but the greatest. Folks may not have agreed with his beliefs, but they couldn't deny his skill.

More than any other athlete, Muhammad Ali defined the 1960s. His life crossed the major political events of the age, including the Vietnam War. In 1964, the military lowered the passing score for the intelligence exams, making Ali eligible for service in the Vietnam War.

Then, on February 17, 1966, the Louisville draft board denied any requests to defer his service. Ali couldn't understand why the army was after him. As a Muslim, he did not believe in war. Enlisting was against his religion. Moreover, he was in the prime of his boxing career. If he stopped to fight the war in Vietnam, there was a chance he would lose years of training or even come back to the United States wounded.

His friend Sugar Ray Robinson tried to convince Ali to just comply. He advised him that there was no way he could get out of it without going to jail. Sugar Ray even suggested that because of Ali's status, he would never have to participate in any actual combat. Ali knew the consequences of saying no to the United States government was jail time. But the consequences of disobeying Elijah could mean a harsher, perhaps violent, punishment. Once again, Ali would favor Elijah over everything. He decided to refuse his military service.

Ali would not fight in Vietnam, nor would he perform in any boxing exhibition there. He spoke out against the war whenever he could. "If I thought going to war would bring freedom and equality to twenty-two million of my people, they wouldn't have to draft me. I'd join tomorrow." Ali believed that it was wrong to fight a war against the Vietnamese while Black people were being attacked in the United States. He posed a question to America: The Vietnamese people didn't do anything to harm Black Americans, so why should a Black man fight over there instead of fighting against mistreatment here at home? On April 20, 1967, Ali officially refused to be inducted into the United States Armed Forces. He declared that it was against his religion.

Almost immediately, the New York State Athletic Commission suspended his boxing license and withdrew his heavyweight title as punishment. Athletic commissions across the country followed suit, forbidding him to box in any ring in America. Months later, the federal court convicted him of draft evasion, a formal charge for people who refuse to serve their country during wartime. They sentenced him to five years in prison and a $10,000 fine. Ali would appeal the decision. He did not have to go to jail, but for nearly four years, he was still banned from the ring. The government clearly intended to send Ali a message.

Without boxing, Ali could not earn as much money as usual. He also wasn't able to book paid appearances at events or on television to earn a living. Ali had been recast as "America's enemy." Very few people wanted to give him a platform. During this punishing time, Ali needed support. But his Muslim brothers were absent. After all the sacrifices he had made for the Nation of Islam, they did not take care of him when he fell on hard times.

As Ali became increasingly frustrated with his situation, he revealed that he was nearly broke and would go back to boxing if the price was right. When Elijah heard him talk about his finances so crudely, he was angry. He suspended Ali for placing "his hopes and trust in the enemy of Allah [white sponsors] for survival." To Elijah, Ali had publicly announced that he would sacrifice his religious beliefs for money, so he decided to harshly punish the fighter. The Messenger suspended Ali from the Nation of Islam and no longer recognized him as a Muslim, even giving him back the name "Cassius Clay." Ali was now experiencing the same cruel isolation that had been used to punish Malcolm X. And, like Malcolm, when Elijah suspended him, Ali was devastated. He hoped that he would soon be forgiven and welcomed back into the Nation. However, Ali was not their prized member. Without boxing, he couldn't raise money or create interest in the Nation, which meant that Ali was no longer valuable to Elijah.

During Ali's exile from boxing, in the immediate years after Malcolm's murder, a cloud of suspicion followed Elijah Muhammad and the Nation of Islam. Reporters, activists, and former members of the Nation believed that the Black Muslims had killed Malcolm.

On February 17, 1966, the same day the armed services announced their decision to recruit Muhammad Ali, a New York judge sentenced Talmadge X and two other members of the Nation to life in prison for the murder of Malcolm X. Talmadge had confessed his involvement in the assassination, but the other two men insisted they were innocent. Talmadge agreed that the two men, Thomas 15X and Norman 3X, were innocent. He never revealed the names of his accomplices. The trial surrounding the murder of Malcolm X seemed to be over, but the spirit of Malcolm X continued to haunt Ali and the Nation of Islam.

Ali fought the draft evasion charges all the way to the Supreme Court, the highest court in the land. In 1971, the justices unanimously ruled in his favor, overturning his draft evasion conviction on a technicality. This ruling marked the beginning of a few important celebrations for

Muhammad Ali. In 1974, he regained the heavyweight title from George Foreman in Zaire, the country now known as the Democratic Republic of the Congo. Thousands of fans greeted Ali in Kinshasa, and he was happy to be celebrated again. It had been a somber few years since Malcolm was assassinated. Ali was controlled by Elijah and trapped under the Nation's surveillance. He couldn't eat, sleep, or travel without the Nation tracing his every move. Ali confided in a reporter that he would have left the Nation had he not witnessed Malcolm's demise. After all those years, it was clear not only that Ali cared about his friend but that the tragedy had scared him to his core. He admitted, "I would have gotten out of this a long time ago, but you saw what they did to Malcolm X....I can't leave the Muslims. They'd shoot me, too."

On February 25, 1975, just a few months after Ali celebrated his reclaimed heavyweight title, Elijah Muhammad died. His son Wallace took over the Nation and established a new order. He declared that his father was neither a "messenger" nor a holy man. He veered away from the Nation's violent, separatist language and also paved the way for a more traditional practice of Islam.

Later, the new Nation renamed Harlem's Mosque

No. 7 to Masjid Malcolm Shabazz in honor of Malcolm X. It acknowledged that Malcolm had told the truth about Elijah's misdeeds and called for the Nation to change. Wallace envisioned an organization that was free of fear and intimidation and open to courage and honesty.

Within the next few years, Malcolm X became a global icon. The Nation of Islam lost thousands of members, and as a result their influence dwindled in the Black community. As the public began digging into the muddled facts surrounding the minister's assassination, they found that a few of the men in Malcolm's circle were secretly FBI informants. While the Nation of Islam was losing credibility, the memory of Malcolm X was gaining appreciation and respect.

In the years after Malcolm's death, his message of Black empowerment became the Black Power movement. This movement promoted racial pride, unity, and self-sufficiency. Young radical Black leaders emerged, emphasizing Black Power and echoing Malcolm's battle cry "by any means necessary." In 1966, Huey Newton and Bobby Seale founded the Black Panther Party. The group established programs to help feed their communities and offered protection from police harassment and abuse. Hugely popular, this grassroots social movement was led by a new generation heavily influenced by Malcolm X.

By the 1970s, the Black Power movement had taken root in popular culture. From political engagement to music, marginalized communities acted and inspired the world to fight the power—or fight for freedom. The legacy of Malcolm X carried on in the decades after his death. His name is now on boulevards in Harlem and Washington, DC. His portrait appears on merchandise of all sorts—from posters to T-shirts and stickers—as a lasting pop culture symbol.

As Malcolm X once said, "So early in life, I had learned that if you want something, you had better make some noise." This message has resonated with generations of Black and brown people and can be seen at work today in the global Black Lives Matter movement: a direct call to action birthed by the tragic deaths of unarmed Black people in the United States. Malcolm's legacy is reflected in countless contemporary human rights and justice movements across the world.

Once Elijah was gone in 1975, Muhammad Ali was free. He announced that he had no time to hate people on any racial basis—this stance was all in the past. He adopted a more hopeful view on race relations and practiced traditional Islam. Ali was about forty years old when he finally retired from boxing. His face and body showed the battle scars of a man who'd spent his youth fighting. He'd become an American icon, representing courage and free will. Many had forgotten about the period when Ali was condemned as "America's nightmare." The outright hatred he provoked by choosing his religion over his country—that controversy felt very much in the past. It seemed that with time the public chose to remember the good and forget about the bad times.

Now that he was older and more secure in his accomplishments and his identity, Muhammad Ali opened up about his true feelings regarding his mentor: "Malcolm X was a great thinker and even greater friend," he reflected.

Forty years after Malcolm's assassination, Ali still lived in regret. He said, "I wish I'd been able to tell Malcolm I was sorry, that he was right about so many things....If I could go back and do it over again, I would never have turned my back on him."

Malcolm and Ali would forever be known as blood brothers. Their friendship was unlikely, but it was vital. Ali was a young champion eager to make a name for himself. As Cassius Clay, he shook up the boxing world and created his own rules. As Muhammad Ali, he garnered international fame and proved that he really was the greatest.

Malcolm X commanded respect as soon as anyone heard him speak. He dreamed of freedom for all Black people by any means necessary. He told young Cassius that he could create his own path to success. He saw something great in Cassius and nurtured it until Cassius truly believed in himself. Malcolm's words and ideas may have shaped who Cassius became, but it was Elijah Muhammad who anointed him as Muhammad Ali, establishing him as "the greatest."

Despite the way history unfolded, Ali never felt as close to Elijah as he had been with Malcolm. And once Malcolm died, Ali hid from his grief by hurling insults at his former friend. Years later, once the hate was gone, Muhammad Ali saw the truth for himself. Ali eventually followed the same path—religious and political—that Malcolm had pioneered. It took years for Ali to understand the meaning behind what Malcolm was trying to teach him. But everything he learned and every greatness he achieved were shaped by his friendship with Malcolm. He knew that without Malcolm X, he would never have become Muhammad Ali.

*   *   *

On June 2, 2016, Muhammad Ali was admitted to an Arizona hospital, suffering from a neurological disease. For the past few years, his health had been declining and the media reported he would not live much longer. Ali had lost the ability to speak and sometimes lost awareness or consciousness. Years before, he had been diagnosed with Parkinson's disease, an illness that affects the central nervous system. Ali was in his early seventies, but the condition made him seem much older, and he took a turn for the worse while in the hospital. His family gathered around to peacefully say goodbye. Ali had lived a great life and was beloved as an icon around the world.

On June 3, 2016, Muhammad Ali died. Athletes, celebrities, and presidents all took time to celebrate how Ali had changed history. They spoke about his courage and confidence. President Barack Obama paid tribute by repeating Ali's words from more than forty years before: "I am America. I am the part you won't recognize. But get used to me—Black, confident, cocky; my name, not yours; my religion, not yours; my goals, my own. Get used to me." It was a powerful statement that supported the independent spirit the boxer exemplified. The traits people had criticized Ali for during his lifetime were now the very same things they praised after his death.

Ali had become more popular when he split from the Nation of Islam. The Nation he'd known was now led by Louis Farrakhan, who previously went by Louis X. Louis revived the very same beliefs held by Elijah Muhammad. By the 1980s, Ali was publicly criticizing Farrakhan and spoke about a universal Muslim brotherhood. If Ali would have stayed loyal to Louis, he would never have become such an international hero. He likely would not have received the honor of lighting the Olympic torch in Atlanta in 1996 or been awarded the Presidential Medal of Freedom. If he had followed Farrakhan, Malcolm X's eldest daughter, Attallah Shabazz, would not have spoken kind words at Ali's funeral.

The fighter's importance to the Shabazz family did not end with Malcolm's death. Ali sought forgiveness through Malcolm's daughters, and Attallah helped him find "the light of understanding." Like Malcolm, Attallah forged an unlikely relationship with Muhammad Ali. Their shared pain and grief became a comfort to each of them. Attallah revealed that her father had forgiven Ali for turning his back on him. Malcolm knew why Ali felt he had to do it. In turn, Ali helped Attallah better understand her dad. Attallah was six years old when she witnessed her father's assassination. Ali was able to tell her stories about her father that she had never heard. Their relationship healed so much pain.

"From the very moment we found one another," Attallah said, "it was as if no time had passed at all, despite all the presumptions of division. Despite all the efforts at separation. Despite all the organized distancing." Her veiled reference to the Nation of Islam suggested that she understood the burden Ali carried as a loyal disciple of Elijah Muhammad.

Attallah's eulogy showed that Malcolm and Ali's bond had never broken. It was a journey of two unlikely friends who found brotherhood despite the chaos and violence of their surroundings. Their friendship traveled a long, bumpy road that ended with healing. Although Ali had once considered Malcolm his enemy, their bond as blood brothers would overcome the deep feelings of betrayal and grief. In the end, forgiveness overcame hate.

ACKNOWLEDGMENTS

From the first stages of our work on *Muhammad Ali and Malcolm X: The Fatal Friendship* we have benefited from the advice and hard work of an incredible group. At Basic Books, Lara Heimert signed and then shepherded *Blood Brothers*, the adult version of the book, through publication. Lara has long been a champion of our writing, and we are thankful for her faith in us. Publisher Christy Ottaviano recognized that the story of Muhammad Ali and Malcolm X was relevant for a younger generation of readers. Many of the racial battles that the two men fought and the barriers that they overcame in the 1960s still exist today. We are grateful for Christy's enthusiasm and the support of her entire team, especially editor Jessica Anderson. We could not have had a better editor than Jessica as we navigated the process of transforming the adult book into a story for young readers. We also wish to thank Margeaux Weston for adapting the book for children. We could not have done it without her.

Finally, Melissa Chinchillo, our literary agent at Fletcher & Company, helped us in more ways than we can count. We owe her—and will continue to owe her—an enormous debt.

—Randy Roberts and Johnny Smith

SELECTED BIBLIOGRAPHY

GOVERNMENT DOCUMENTS

Federal Bureau of Investigation, US Department of
    Justice files

        Muhammad Ali

        Leon Phillips (Aka Leon Ameer)

        Malcolm X Little

        Elijah Muhammad

        Nation of Islam

ARCHIVAL COLLECTIONS

George Barry Bingham Papers, Filson Historical Society,
    Louisville, KY

Alex Haley papers, Manuscripts, Archives and Rare Books
    Division, Schomburg Center for Research in Black
    Culture, New York Public Library, New York, NY

Jack Olsen papers, University of Oregon Special
    Collections and Archives

Malcolm X papers, Manuscripts, Archives and Rare Books
Division, Schomburg Center for Research in Black
Culture, New York Public Library, New York, NY

NEWSPAPERS

Baltimore Afro-American

Chicago Defender

Chicago Sun-Times

Chicago Tribune

Los Angeles Sentinel

Los Angeles Times

Louisville Courier-Journal

Daily Mirror (London)

Las Vegas Sun

Miami Herald

Muhammad Speaks

New York Amsterdam News

Daily News (New York)

New York Herald Tribune

New York Post

New York Times

Pittsburgh Courier

The Times (London)

Washington Post

MAGAZINE ARTICLES

"A Wet Way to Train for a Fight." *Life*, September 8, 1961.

Barbee, Bobbie E. "Will Link with Malcolm X Harm Clay's Career?" *Jet*, March 26, 1964.

Boyle, Robert H. "This Is What Clay Says He Wants." *Sports Illustrated*, August 5, 1963.

Brennan, Michael. "Ali and His Educators." *Sports Illustrated*, September 22, 1980.

"Cassius Clay Says: 'I'm Tired of Fighting Unrated Bums!!' " *The Ring*, February 1962.

"Cassius X." *Newsweek*, March 16, 1964.

"Champ's African 'Love Affair.' " *Ebony*, September 1964.

Cope, Myron. "Muslim Champ." *Saturday Evening Post*, November 14, 1964.

Gottehrer, Barry. "How Cassius Clay Tricked the World." *Sport*, June 1964.

Haley, Alex. "Alex Haley Remembers Malcolm X." *Essence*, November 1983.

Hamill, Pete. "The Man Who Filled the Garden." *New York Post Magazine*, March 17, 1963.

Horn, Huston. " 'E Said 'E Would and 'E Did." *Sports Illustrated*, July 1, 1963.

———. "The First Days in the New Life of the Champion of the World." *Sports Illustrated*, March 9, 1964.

———. "A Rueful Dream Come True." *Sports Illustrated*, November 18, 1963.

———. "'Who Made Me—Is *Me*!'" *Sports Illustrated*, September 25, 1961.

Kempton, Murray. "Cassius Clay: 'I Whipped Him and I'm Still Pretty.'" *New Republic*, March 7, 1964.

Liebling, A. J. "Anti-Poetry Night." *New Yorker*, March 30, 1963.

———. "Poet and Pedagogue." *New Yorker*, March 3, 1962.

Lipsyte, Robert. "Cassius Clay, Cassius X, Muhammad Ali." *New York Times Magazine*, October 25, 1964.

"Malcolm's Brand X." *Newsweek*, March 23, 1964.

Malcolm X and James Farmer. "Separation or Integration: A Debate." *Dialogue Magazine*, May 1962.

Massaquoi, Hans J. "Mystery of Malcolm X." *Ebony*, September 1964.

Maule, Tex. "Yes, It Was Good and Honest." *Sports Illustrated*, March 9, 1964.

McHugh, Roy. "Can Cassius Clay Win His Big Gamble?" *Sport*, October 1963.

———. "Cassius Clay—He Talks So Big." *Sport*, December 1962.

Morrison, Allan. "Who Killed Malcolm X?" *Ebony*, October 1965.

"Muhammad Ali in Africa." *Sports Illustrated*, June 1, 1964.

Olsen, Jack. "Learning Elijah's Advanced Lesson in Hate." *Sports Illustrated*, May 2, 1966.

Patterson, Floyd, with Milton Gross. "I Want to Destroy Cassius Clay." *Sports Illustrated*, October 19, 1964.

"Playboy Interview: Cassius Clay." *Playboy*, October 1964.

Plimpton, George. "Miami Notebook: Cassius Clay and Malcolm X." *Harper's Magazine*, June 1964.

Poinsett, Alex. "A Look at Cassius Clay: Biggest Mouth in Boxing." *Ebony*, March 1963.

"Prizefighting: Cassius X." *Time*, March 13, 1964.

Samuels, Gertrude. "Two Ways: Black Muslim and N.A.A.C.P." *New York Times Magazine*, May 12, 1963.

Smith, Gary. "Ali and His Entourage." *Sports Illustrated*, April 25, 1988.

Tuckner, Howard. "'Man, It's Great to Be Great.'" *New York Times Magazine*, December 9, 1962.

"Why Malcolm X Quit the Black Muslims." *Sepia*, May 1964.

Wolfe, Tom. "The Marvelous Mouth." *Esquire*, October 1963.

Worthy, William. "The Angriest Negroes." *Esquire*, February 1961.

BOOKS

Ali, Muhammad, with Hana Yasmeen Ali. *The Soul of a Butterfly*. New York: Simon & Schuster, 2004.

Ali, Muhammad, with Richard Durham. *The Greatest: My Own Story*. New York: Random House, 1975.

Atyeo, Don, and Felix Dennis. *Muhammad Ali: The Holy Warrior*. New York: Simon & Schuster, 1975.

Baldwin, James. *The Fire Next Time*. New York: Vintage International, 1993. First published in 1963 by Dial Press.

Bingham, Howard, and Max Wallace. *Muhammad Ali's Greatest Fight: Cassius Clay vs. the United States of America*. New York: M. Evans and Company, Inc., 2000.

Boyd, Herb, and Ilyasah Al-Shabazz, eds. *The Diary of Malcolm X (El-Hajj Malik El-Shabazz): 1964*. Chicago: Third World Press, 2013.

Branch, Taylor. *Parting the Waters: America in the King Years, 1954–1963*. New York: Simon & Schuster, 1989.

———. *Pillar of Fire: America In The King Years, 1963–1965*. New York: Simon & Schuster, 1998.

Breitman, George, ed. *Malcolm X Speaks: Selected Speeches and Statements*. New York: Grove Press, 1990.

Carson, Clayborne. *Malcolm X: The FBI File*. New York: Carrol & Graf, 1991.

Clegg, Claude Andrew. *An Original Man: The Life and Times of Elijah Muhammad*. New York: St. Martin's Press, 1997.

Early, Gerald, ed. *The Muhammad Ali Reader*. New York: Robert Weisbach Books, 1998.

Goldman, Peter. *The Death and Life of Malcolm X*. 2nd ed. Urbana: University of Illinois Press, 1979.

Gorn, Elliot, ed. *Muhammad Ali: The People's Champ*. Urbana: University of Illinois Press, 1995.

Hauser, Thomas. *Muhammad Ali: His Life and Times*. New York: Simon & Schuster, 1991.

Joseph, Peniel. *The Sword and the Shield: The Revolutionary Lives of Malcolm X and Martin Luther King*. New York: Basic Books, 2020.

Malcolm X, as told to Alex Haley. *The Autobiography of Malcolm X*. New York: Ballantine, 1965. Reprint, New York: Ballantine, 1992.

Marable, Manning. *Malcolm X: A Life of Reinvention*. New York: Viking, 2011.

Marable, Manning, and Garret Felber, eds. *The Portable Malcolm X Reader*. New York: Penguin Books, 2013.

Olsen, Jack. *Black Is Best: The Riddle of Cassius Clay*. New York: Dell, 1967.

Perry, Bruce, ed. *Malcolm X: The Last Speeches*. New York: Pathfinder, 1989.

Remnick, David. *King of the World: Muhammad Ali and the Rise of an American Hero*. New York: Viking, 1998.

Rickford, Russell J. *Betty Shabazz: A Remarkable Story of Survival and Faith Before and After Malcolm X*. Naperville, IL: Sourcebooks, Inc., 2003.

Tosches, Nick. *The Devil and Sonny Liston*. Boston: Little, Brown, 2000.

WEBSITES

Zirin, Dave. "Read What Malcolm X's Daughter Said at Muhammad Ali's Funeral." *The Nation*, June 17, 2016. https://www.thenation.com/article/archive/the-words -of-malcolm-xs-daughter-attalah-shabazz-at-muhammad -alis-funeral/.

INDEX

N

NAACP (National Association for the Advancement of Colored People), 85–87, 91–92, 99
Nation of Islam (NOI)
    Ali and. *See* Ali, Muhammad, and Nation of Islam
    "Black racism" of, 38
    Clay family and, 24, 116–19
    Elijah Muhammad and. *See* Muhammad, Elijah
    Johnson X incident, 26–31, 32
    Malcolm X and. *See* Malcolm X
    numerology, 129–30
    opposition to Civil Rights Movement, 39–41
    rise of Malcolm X, 26–41
    separatist ideology of, 2–3, 40, 68–69, 86–87, 102, 201
    true believers of, 31–32
    use of "X," 31–32
New York Amsterdam News, 149–50
New York City newspaper strike, 77
New York City Police Department (NYPD), 100, 186, 187–88, 191–92
New York Post, 178
New York State Athletic Commission, 198
New York State's Joint Legislative Committee on Professional Boxing, 80–81
New York Times, 58, 97
Nigeria, 162, 165
Nkrumah, Kwame, 167–68

O

Obama, Barack, 206
Ole Miss riot of 1962, 84
Olympia Stadium (Detroit), 67–69
Organization of Afro-American Unity (OAAU), 181
Overtown, Miami, 16, 19–21

P

Patterson, Floyd, 144
    Ali as sparring partner, 18
    in Birmingham, 88, 89
    Liston fights, 76, 97–98
    Malcolm's criticism of, 89
police brutality, 12, 66–67
    Johnson X incident, 28–31, 32
    Stokes and Los Angeles police shooting of 1962, 57–64
Presidential Medal of Freedom, 207
Presley, Elvis, 98

Q

Quran, 167

R

racial integration, 3–4, 40, 56, 67, 85–87, 88, 91–92, 99–100, 121, 158
Roberts, Gene, 186–87, 188, 189
Robertson, Oscar, 10
Robinson, Jackie, 80, 88–89
Robinson, Sugar Ray, 80, 127, 149, 197
Roi, Sonji, 177
Rome Olympic Games (1960), 10–11, 17

ABOUT THE AUTHORS

Randy Roberts is the 150th Anniversary Professor and Distinguished Professor of History at Purdue University. In addition to winning the Charles B. Murphy Outstanding Undergraduate Teaching Award at Purdue University and twice receiving Teacher of the Year in the School of Liberal Arts, he was named the Carnegie Foundation for the Advancement of Teaching Indiana Professor of the Year. He specializes in teaching military history, sports history, and popular culture. Roberts is also an award-winning, bestselling author. He has won several national book awards. He has written three books with Johnny Smith. Roberts has frequently served as a consultant and on-camera commentator for PBS, HBO, and the History Channel. Two of the documentaries he was featured in won Emmy Awards. He lives in Lafayette, Indiana, with his wife, Marjie.

Johnny Smith is the Julius C. "Bud" Shaw Professor of Sports History and associate professor of history at Georgia Tech, where he teaches courses about United States history and sports history. Smith is the author of four books, and his next book is *Jumpman: The Making and Meaning of Michael Jordan*. He lives in Atlanta, Georgia.

Margeaux Weston is the author of *20th Century African American History for Kids* and the coauthor of *We Are the United States*, among other books. She is also the nonfiction editor of the Hugo Award–winning *FIYAH Magazine of Black Speculative Fiction*. She is an editor and a book coach, having worked with We Need Diverse Books, among other organizations. Margeaux lives in southern Louisiana with her husband and three boys.